D0893326

WITHDRAWN

PRIVATE THEODORE S. GARNETT
BEFORE HIS PROMOTION TO LIEUTENANT AND AIDE-DE-CAMP

Courtesy of the Author

RIDING WITH STUART

Reminiscences of an Aide-de-Camp

by
Captain Theodore Stanford Garnett

edited by
Robert J. Trout

 White Mane Publishing Co., Inc.

This White Mane Publishing Company, Inc. publication
was printed by
Beidel Printing House, Inc.
63 West Burd Street
Shippensburg, PA 17257 USA

In respect for the scholarship contained herein, the acid-free paper used in this book meets the guidelines for permanence and durability of the Committee on Production Guidelines for Book Longevity of the Council on Library Resources.

For a complete list of available publications
please write
White Mane Publishing Company, Inc.
P.O. Box 152
Shippensburg, PA 17257 USA

Library of Congress Cataloging-in-Publication Data

Garnett, Theodore Stanford, 1844-1915.
    Riding with Stuart : reminiscences of an aide-de-camp / by
Theodore Stanford Garnett : edited by Robert J. Trout.
        p.   cm.
    Includes index.
    ISBN 0-942597-58-3 : $19.95
    1. United States--History--Civil War, 1861-1865--Campaigns.
2. Virginia--History--Civil War, 1861-1865--Campaigns. 3. Garnett,
Theodore Stanford, 1844-1915. 4. Stuart, Jeb, 1833-1864--Friends
and associates. 5. United States--History--Civil War, 1861-1865-
-Personal narratives, Confederate. 6. Virginia--History--Civil War,
1861-1865--Personal narratives, Confederate. 7. Confederate States
of America. Army--Biography. 8. Soldiers--Southern States-
-Biography. I. Trout, Robert J., 1947-   . II. Title.
E475.7.G37 1994
973.7'455--dc20   93-48948
                                                                CIP

PRINTED IN THE UNITED STATES OF AMERICA

This edition is dedicated to
Captain Theodore Stanford Garnett
and to
Major General James E. B. Stuart

— METHODOLOGY —

—   Garnett used a plain line in his original text when he did not remember the date or was unsure. He also used the line to take the place of letters he wished to exclude from a name. Those lines have been left as they are in the original text.

(   )   Parentheses are Garnett's and are in the original text.

[   ]   Brackets enclose information supplied by the editor.

{   }   These different parentheses contain material Garnett wrote in the margins of the manuscript.

Spelling (Garnett made only about twenty-spelling errors in ninety-eight pages of writing) has not been changed with the following exception. Garnett abbreviated many words, especially place names. Some of his abbreviations have been written out in full to avoid the overuse of bracketed explanations or footnotes. Also, paragraph indentations have been inserted in some instances to assist the reader as Garnett often wrote several pages without a new paragraph.

— TABLE OF CONTENTS —

List of Illustrations

Maps

— FOREWORD —

by
Maria Tyler Garnett Hood

As children, my brother, the fifth Theodore Stanford Garnett, and I were mildly pursued by our father to understand our heritage. I was either too young or too liberal in my views at the time to permit instruction about any of my ancestors, especially not those who helped the Confederate cause. My brother was too busy inventing things, writing, drawing, and building models, a definite throw-back to his great-grandfather — to receive explanation on what he knew also was bound to be dry and boring.

Time passed and both of us married and raised families. My nephew is the sixth Theodore Stanford Garnett. Our father, also nicknamed as was his father "The," died in 1986 of a heart attack in Camp Greenbrier in Alderson, West Virginia. He was eighty-one.

Almost immediately, I realized how little I knew of an accurate family background. This ignorance was in spite of my grandfather's passion for The War Between the States and my father's dedicated record keeping of family history and genealogy. I had seen bits and pieces of memorabilia stuck in odd places about our home for years. Also by this time, our once bright and inquisitive mother was suffering from severe memory loss. Her condition and the fact that much of our history had died with my father was a sad realization.

My brother and I were then forced to close the family home in Norfolk, Virginia. At the end of that difficult day of dividing the beloved contents of our home, we faced the garage, the place where all miscellaneous and generally worthless articles are stored until the time when fading memory allows you to pitch them. Both mental and physical fatigue had brought the two of us to the pitching point. We dutifully hauled from the rafters dust covered boxes disintegrating from decades of mouse inhabitants. We vacillated between throwing it all out on the spot or going box by box through what appeared to be a worthless mess. Fortunately, at the top of one of the first boxes was a small leather diary with dates beginning in 1866, the year after the war. My brother dug deeper and found what looked like real treasures from the Civil War. Apparently we had stumbled upon materials inherited by our father from his father. It was decided that I should keep everything together and carry it to my home on the Eastern Shore of Virginia where I could go through the boxes when time allowed.

After a time, I took the first diary we had found and gave it to a friend, Brooks Miles Barnes, who is a well respected historian on the Eastern Shore. He informed me that we had fallen upon significant material. To my questions concerning the validity and importance of the diary, he laughed, "Maria, the man was Fitz Lee's groomsman for heaven's sake." It was through Miles's urging that I began my trek through the boxes of diaries and notes, most of which I discovered in excellent condition. Those that were written by an earlier "The" were easy to read, for his handwriting was artistic and clear. His brother James's diaries (I remember the family referring to him as "Dismal Jimmy") were almost impossible to decipher. So beautiful the writing of "The's," however, it was clear to me why he had been assigned as clerk to General Stuart.

Not until the fall of 1988 did I reach the bottom of the box to find what was the second half of war memoirs. The original manuscript was written in a hard backed, lined book which had evidently doubled as a law course notebook. Its legal size had decided its position in the box. So fascinating were the contents to me that when I began to read, I only stopped once before completing it. I read parts to my husband, my children, and anyone who would listen. I realized I was doing a little of what my father had done to me some thirty years before. This time, however, there was a difference. So captivating were the vignettes that my children listened.

Believing that such information belonged to more than just our family, I eagerly presented, in behalf of my parents, brother, and me, all the materials found in the box to the Alderman Library, University of Virginia. These diaries and manuscripts were added to the Mercer-Garnett collection housed at the library. At the time of presentation, Robert Trout, the man responsible for the publication of this book, was present at my invitation, for he was in the process of writing a book on Stuart's staff. His enthusiasm and knowledge gave me insight into the value of my great-grandfather's work which illuminates a small slice of our history.

THEODORE S. GARNETT, SR.
FATHER OF "THE"
Courtesy of Mrs. Maria Hood

MRS. THEODORE S. GARNETT, SR.
MOTHER OF "THE"
Courtesy of Mrs. Maria Hood

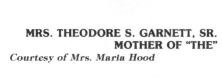

EMILY EYRE BAKER
WIFE OF T. S. GARNETT
Courtesy of Mrs. Maria Hood

Part I

Theodore Sanford Garnett:
A Biography

THERE ARE MANY criteria by which a general officer measures the individuals he wishes to add to his staff. Courage, stamina, talent, and personality are but a few of the requirements that play a role in the selection process. Sometimes the capability of performing a rather common task extremely well makes one man stand above another. Such a capability brought Theodore Stanford Garnett, Jr., to cavalry headquarters and eventually to the staff of Major General James Ewell Brown "Jeb" Stuart.

In May of 1863, Stuart wrote the Confederate Secretary of the Navy, Stephen R. Mallory, asking him for a recommendation to fill a clerk's position at Stuart's cavalry headquarters. That individual had to be both trustworthy and able to write with a rapid and legible hand, legibility being of major importance. Mallory did not need to search far because his own nephew, "The" Garnett, met Stuart's conditions in every respect. On May 15, 1863 Garnett went through the formality of enlisting in Company F, 9th Virginia Cavalry and then immediately reported to Stuart.

Garnett arrived at cavalry headquarters just before the beginning of the summer campaign and quickly demonstrated a desire to serve his commander in any way. Born in Richmond on October 28, 1844 Garnett was the son of Theodore S. Garnett and his wife, the former Florentina Isidora Moreno of Pensacola, Florida. When young Garnett was ten, his family moved to Hanover County, and he began attending Episcopal High School in Alexandria, Virginia. The outbreak of the war brought Garnett home where he quickly enlisted in Captain William Nelson's "Hanover Artillery." The company eventually marched to Richmond to be mustered into the Confederate service and at that juncture Garnett met with a rude shock.

The mustering officer took one look at the thin, sixteen year old and rejected him on the grounds that he was too young. Garnett objected to no avail and along with two of his equally young and rejected companions sought out President Jefferson Davis's military advisor, General Robert E. Lee, to plead their case. Lee listened intently but told the three to go back to their homes.

Completely dejected, Garnett felt he had to do something. His sole recourse was to accept a clerkship from his "Uncle Mallory" in the Navy Department offices in Richmond. For the next eighteen months he performed the mundane tasks associated with his position until Stuart's request liberated him. Even though his assignment would still involve being a clerk, Garnett quickly proved to Stuart that he had talents other than penmanship.

In the days that followed Garnett's arrival at cavalry headquarters, the Army of Northern Virginia began the maneuvers which ultimately led to the Battle of Gettysburg. Stuart's cavalry fought at Brandy Station, Aldie, Middleburg, and Upperville, Virginia, and at Hanover, Pennsylvania. Many other smaller skirmishes occurred, and Garnett managed to put himself under his general's eye while acting as scout and courier. Stuart soon began to appreciate the varied skills which Garnett displayed, including that of foraging.

The Confederate cavalry's long ride to Pennsylvania exhausted both men and horses. Lieutenant Frank S. Robertson, one of Stuart's engineer officers, found himself in need of a new mount and, seeing that Garnett's horse was in the same condition, suggested that they attempt to secure fresh transportation. Leaving the security of the column was dangerous, but the two rode off into the nearby woods. Their search through the brush led to the discovery of a dozen or more horses obviously hidden to avoid exactly what was about to take place. A rapid exchange of saddle, blanket, and other accouterments and the two horsetraders were soon back with the rest of the cavalry.

Garnett described his experiences after the close of the Gettysburg Campaign up to June, 1864, including his appointment as Stuart's aide-de-camp, in the memoir that follows. His subsequent service as aide to Major General William Henry Fitzhugh Lee eventually brought him a promotion to captain on March 1, 1865 and assignment as assistant adjutant general on the staff of Brigadier General William P. Roberts. In a letter to the Richmond *Times-Dispatch* written on April 7, 1905 Garnett told of his last day as a soldier before his surrender at Appomattox Court House.

> Riding back [Garnett had just turned over some prisoners captured on April 8, 1865] I met Genl. Roberts coming towards the Court House, and he asked me if I had heard any rumor of our surrender. I replied "no" — and the question at the moment struck me as quite absurd. But seeing the General's expression of countenance was serious, I asked him "What do you mean?" His reply was: "General Lee is going to surrender this Army. I have just received orders to leave here and march to Buckingham C.H. where Genl. Fitz Lee says the cavalry will rendezvous."
>
> Directing me to take our little remnant of the brigade off the field, Genl. Roberts left me for a few moments. I passed a few hundred yards West of the Court House and struck a trot with the column, soon

reaching a good road, and pushed on towards Buckingham. The General re-joined us a short distance Northwest of the Court House and we fell into a walk, a silent and solemn procession of about 100 men, but men who were ready to obey any order and would be faithful unto death.

We had gone about two miles in this way when Maj. Robt. Mason of Genl. Fitz Lee's Staff, overtook us and said that Genl. Fitz Lee wished the column halted to await his coming. I gathered from this message that Genl. Fitz Lee wanted to give us some parting instructions or to say "farewell" to the men. Arriving on top of a hill, I faced the men into line on the right of the road looking back towards the Court House — and in a short time Genl. Fitz Lee arrived. Genl. Roberts rode to meet him — and soon returned, ordering me to disband the brigade, — which I did in these words:

"Men, Genl. Roberts says you can break ranks and disband. We bid you good bye, and you may go back to North Carolina in any way you choose."

Unclasping my sabre from my belt I threw it far from me, so as to let the men know that I, at least, considered the war at an end.

In two minutes there was not a man to be seen, and General Roberts, his Adjutant General [Garnett] and courier Forbes were left there, the sole representatives of Robert's Cavalry Brigade.

Garnett was paroled on April 21, 1865.

In the fall of 1865 Garnett entered the University of Virginia to study law. He graduated in 1867 and attempted to establish a practice in Warrenton, supporting himself in the meantime by teaching in a private school. His efforts proved fruitless, and in 1869 he moved to Norfolk though he set up his law office in nearby Suffolk. In 1870 he was elected judge of Nansemond, a position he held for three years. Declining reelection he returned to Norfolk and formed a law partnership with William H. White which lasted until Garnett's death.

Garnett was active in the United Confederate Veterans and attended their reunions and other functions. In 1900 he took command of the 1st Brigade of the Virginia Division of the organization with the rank of brigadier general. Elected to major general in 1906 to command the entire Virginia Division, he eventually rose to the rank of lieutenant general in charge of the Confederate Veterans Department of Virginia. He also served on the committee to erect a statue of Stuart in Richmond and gave the speech at its dedication.

In addition to his law practice and involvement in the Confederate Veterans Garnett was made a trustee of both the Virginia Theological Seminary and his old school, Episcopal High School. He was elected into the Alpha Chapter of Phi Beta Kappa at the College of William and Mary, and served as a member of the State Library Board.

On April 27, 1915 Garnett died at his home in Norfolk. His death was due to blood poisoning following a routine tooth extraction. He had been married twice. His first wife was Emily Eyre Baker of Norfolk and his second wife was Louise Bowdoin of Northampton County, Virginia. He was survived by his second wife, a daughter, Lelia, a son, Theodore, Jr., five grandchildren, and two step-children. Garnett was buried in Elmwood Cemetery in Norfolk.

Part II

Introduction to the Reminiscences

THE FIGURE OF Major General Jeb Stuart looms large in the history of the gallant Army of Northern Virginia. Along with General Robert E. Lee and Lieutenant General Thomas J. "Stonewall" Jackson, Stuart has become the subject of numerous biographers and historians.

In Stuart's case, writers were drawn to the memoirs, reminiscences, letters, and articles penned by those who were closest to Stuart — the members of his staff. Several of the cavalry chieftain's staff officers recorded their impressions of Stuart and the life of a Confederate cavalry officer in camp and on campaign. William W. Blackford's *War Years With Jeb Stuart*, Heros von Borcke's *Memoirs of the Confederate War*, John Esten Cooke's *Wearing of the Gray* and *Outlines from the Outpost* (to name but two of his many works) and Henry B. McClellan's *I Rode With Jeb Stuart* became the standard references for those wishing to experience riding with Stuart. The letters of Peter W. Hairston, Philip H. Powers, R. Channing Price, Frank S. Robertson, and J. Hardeman Stuart and the diaries of Cooke, J. Hardeman Stuart, and Alexander R. Boteler help clarify the picture of one who has been called "the best cavalryman ever foaled in North America."[1]

With such a wealth of primary source material it would seem that the years between 1861 and 1864 have been documented completely as far as Stuart is concerned. However, many officers served on the staff at relatively the same time, and their letters and reminiscences recount the same events from the individual's perspective. While that is most helpful to the researcher, gaps in the record do exist because an officer had either gone on furlough, been wounded or killed, or simply left the staff. Not being able to study a certain time period through the eyes of one who was there leaves the historian to tiptoe gently around the events of that period or to attempt a reconstruction of what might have happened by extrapolating from the few facts available. Therefore, historians feel great excitement when a new, primary source of information which clarifies one of these "lost" periods is discovered in some dusty archive or dark attic. Theodore Stanford Garnett's *Continuation of War Sketches* is such a document.

The period of the war covered in *Continuation of War Sketches* (October 1863 to June 1864) begins with an account of the Confederate cavalry's role during the Bristoe Station Campaign from October 9 to November 9, 1863.

Garnett then recounts the cavalry's attempt to settle into winter quarters and provides an intimate, behind the scenes view of the encampment near Orange Court House including the most detailed description of a cavalry headquarters encampment to be found anywhere. The staff's settling in process was interrupted between November 26 and December 2, 1863 by Federal Major General George G. Meade's Mine Run Campaign, and Garnett tells of the cavalry's participation in that repulse of the Union army. Garnett did not overlook the personnel surrounding Stuart nor such moments as the Christmas season serenading of the ladies of Orange Court House by the headquarters band. In late February 1864 the war again forced Stuart to leave his comfortable quarters and ride off in pursuit of the Kilpatrick-Dahlgren raiders who attempted to penetrate Richmond's defenses and free Union prisoners. Finally, Garnett writes of the Wilderness-Spotsylvania Campaign in May 1864 and of his commander's ride to Yellow Tavern. Throughout the memoir Garnett misses little that Stuart aficionados would care to know. Even the tragic moments of Stuart's mortal wounding, death, and burial are illuminated by a still deeply moved Garnett though these sections of his memoir were written four decades after the events occurred.[2]

While the cavalry's operations in that period do not command the interest of historians as much as some earlier periods, the interval is quite intriguing for those who focus their attention on Stuart because very little has been written about this time by the major Stuart chroniclers. Of those mentioned only Blackford, Boteler, Cooke, McClellan, and Robertson were still on the staff.[3] Among this group Boteler was involved on military court martial duties which kept him from close contact with Stuart; Robertson was recuperating from his physical collapse after the Gettysburg Campaign and was not present; and in his writings McClellan chose to concentrate on military aspects at the expense of the personal and camplife side of Stuart and cavalry headquarters. Cooke and Blackford were in a position to write about what transpired, but Cooke apparently found little to romanticize and virtually ignored these months while Blackford briefly mentioned them in passing on to his promotion and assignment to the Confederate Engineer regiments then being formed.[4] Garnett's recently discovered reminiscence is the only account by a staff member during this time, and it does not disappoint the reader.

The title of Garnett's narrative and the initial passages of the memoir pose a tantalizing mystery. Clearly they infer that another "War Sketch" was penned previous to this one and may have covered the months from Garnett's first attachment to cavalry headquarters in May 1863 to October 1863. After reading *Continuation of War Sketches* one can only hope that its lost predecessor can be found. Until that time satisfaction can be drawn from the fact that a new and intimate portrait of Lee's cavalry chief, of the men who rode with him, and of their life during the turmoil of war has been uncovered and made available to those who still ride with Stuart in spirit.

MAJOR GENERAL J.E.B. STUART
Courtesy of The Valentine Museum
Richmond, Virginia

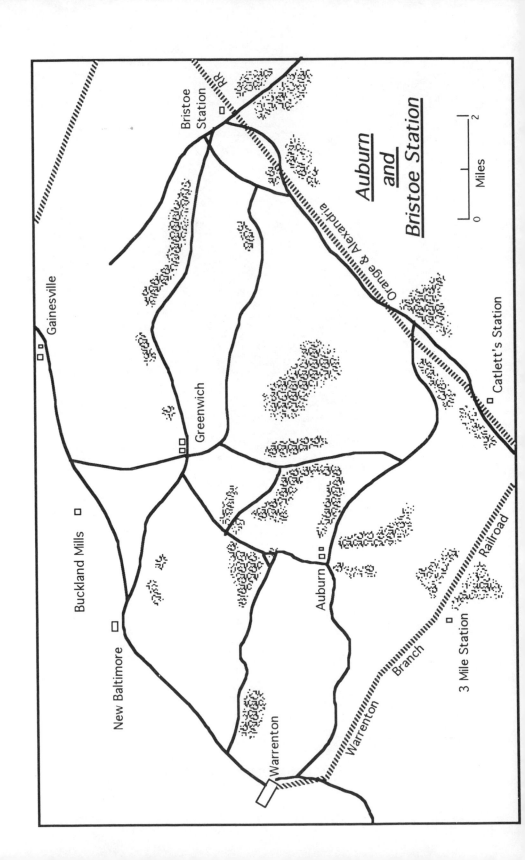

Auburn
and
Bristoe Station

Continuation of War Sketches

I WILL NOT undertake to give any account of the campaign alluded to above (Bristoe). A rapid glance at the movement of our cavalry will suffice. Genl. Fitz [Major General Fitzhugh] Lee crossed the Rapidan at Raccoon Ford on the morning of the _____ day of October, 1863, with [Brigadier General Williams C.] Wickham's and [Brigadier General James B.] Gordon's Brigades. A severe fight immediately ensued, resulting in the rapid retreat of the enemy cavalry in the direction of Stevensburg. I think it was during this engagement that a little incident occurred which created some merriment at the expense of a certain captain in the 1st North Carolina Cavalry [Brigadier General Rufus] (Barringer). His squadron was not engaged, but drawn up on the field waiting orders, and exposed to a heavy artillery fire. Gen. Gordon sent him word to retire to the south side of the river and get out of range. As the captain rode out in front of his squadron to give the order for the execution of this maneuver, a shell from one of the enemy's guns came screaming over and burst just above his head. In the utmost haste, he yelled out at the top of his voice, "By shells! Right about wheel!" which order the men were satisfied could only mean, "By fours," and accordingly lost no time in executing it.

Gen. [Major General James Ewell Brown] Stuart, with [Major General Wade] Hampton and [Brigadier General Pierce Manning Butler] Young, had met the enemy cavalry not far from Culpeper Court House and was driving them toward Brandy Station. Putting himself in communication with Genl. Fitz Lee, who had reached Stevensburg, the two columns moved rapidly on to our old fighting ground around Brandy Station. Here a general engagement ensued, more hotly contested perhaps than any we had ever before fought there. The green fields and lovely meadows which are here spread out in magnificent expanse in front of John Minor Botts', Kennedy's, and Wise's were once more, and for the last time I believe, made the scene of hostile encounter. Charge after charge was made in rapid succession, battery after battery brought into action, until the whole available force of both sides was joined in the awful fray. Toward night, however, by a sweeping charge along the whole line, in some instances whole commands charging by regimental front, the enemy's line was broken and went off in full retreat across the Rappahannock River.[1] {Side notation: Review this!}

Pushing on the next day, Genl. Stuart found himself in advance of our infantry, and on the flank of the enemy as they were moving toward Manassas.

Arriving at Auburn with two brigades of cavalry and [Captain William Morrell] McGregor's Battery of artillery, he determined to make a reconnoisance [sic] of the enemy's line which was moving along the Orange and Alexandria Railroad.[2] Halting the column at Auburn, a little hamlet in Fauquier County, he inspected the enemy with his field glasses at his leisure. But what was his astonishment when a courier rode up and informed him that a similar column of the enemy was passing a few hundred yards in his rear on a road parallel with the railroad. Ordering the men to keep as quiet as possible, but to be prepared for either a fight or a footrace, he determined to remain where he was, hemmed in by the dense masses of Yankee infantry, cavalry, and artillery moving on each side and within pistol shot of his brave little command. It was not long before he was assured that the enemy were ignorant of his situation, as they kept trampling by as steadily and in a manner as unconcerned as if these 1500 Confederate cavalry were 1000 miles away. But how long could this state of things continue? The rattling of a sabre, or the neighing of a horse could be distinctly heard by the enemy, and chances of being discovered by some straggler from their column amounted almost to a certainty. But the night set in and they were still undiscovered. Later and later it grew, every hour seeming doubled in length to the anxious watchers and still the swarming masses of the enemy streamed by, the stifled hum of their voices, the heavy tramp of men and horses, and the rough jostling of artillery and wagons distinctly audible to every man in Stuart's ranks.

During the night the Genl. thought it necessary to inform General [Robert E.] Lee of his situation. Sending to McGregor's Battery, which was posted nearest the enemy, for volunteers to go on this perilous mission, a young man named Chichester (I think), was the first to respond to the call, and giving him a verbal message to the Genl. comd'g, who was expected somewhere near Warrenton, he started him off. The message reached Gen. Lee safely, Chichester having slipped thro' the enemy's ranks in the darkness and gone on his way rejoicing.

This exploit was repeated by two or three others, whose names I have forgotten, and Gen. Lee was supplied with accurate information during the night.[3] When day dawned the enemy's rearguard, one brigade of infantry, had passed by and gone into camp not a quarter of a mile from where Gen. Stuart's command had passed the night. It was the work of an instant only to run out McGregor's Battery and open a brisk fire on them as they busied themselves around their newly made campfires making their morning cup of coffee. The first shell fell among them like a clap of thunder in a clear sky. They rushed to their arms and formed in time to receive the charge of the 1st North Carolina Cavalry under the gallant Gordon, which they repulsed by a heavy volley, but broke and scattered away like sheep immediately after delivering it. Another charge was made which would have resulted in the capture of the whole command but for the intervention of a deep ditch across which they had retreated and over which the cavalry could not go. One brigade of our infantry then joined Gen. Stuart, but it was too late, the enemy, profiting by their experience, had hurried away and regained their main body.

The General after alluded to this little affair, and acknowledged it to be one of his remarkably "tight places."[4]

[Major General George G.] Meade's Army reached the fortifications around Manassas before General Lee could strike him a single blow. The only thing to be done then was to return to our lines on the Rapidan. This was done in the most leisurely manner, and without serious accident, save in one instance, at Rappahannock Bridge, where [Brigadier General Harry T.] Hays' Louisiana Brigade, by some unaccountable blunder on somebody's part, was almost entirely captured.[5]

On the return, Genl. Stuart had an opportunity to settle some old scores with Gen. [Brigadier General Hugh J.] Kilpatrick. Leaving Fitz Lee's Division in Prince William County, and falling back before Kilpatrick, he drew the enemy on towards Buckland. Halting a few miles south of Buckland, he assumed the offensive, and sending word to Fitz Lee to come up with all speed on Kilpatrick's flank, he charged his front with such spirit and vigor as to throw him into confusion. Then pressing on, he was greeted by the sound of Fitz Lee's guns and the cheers of his men as they dashed upon the retreating Yankees. The result was that the whole of Kilpatrick's Division was routed and he himself narrowly escaped capture by leaping his horse over a garden fence in the town of Buckland.[6]

The return to the line of the Rapidan River was then leisurely effected, and the end of the month (October) saw our whole army back in its place distributed along the south bank of the Rapidan from the neighborhood of Germanna Ford on the right to Barnett's [Ford] on the left, a distance of some 15 or 20 miles.

About the 3rd of November, 1863, I was sufficiently recovered to return to camp, and accordingly started to join the General. Reaching Orange Court House I made my way out to Headquarters which was located in a pleasant valley about a mile and a half northeast of town. Here sheltered from the north wind by a sloping hill thickly studded with a forest of cedar and pine on one side and oak on the other, with plenty of water and good grass for our horses we entered upon a winter of quiet contentment unbroken except by occasional expeditions against the enemy. How shall I tell of all that happened during those glorious November days thro' whose mellow sunlight we looked back upon the toils and losses as well as the joys and glories of the past campaign. The greater part of the month was consumed in building winter quarters. The

— 15 —

camp was laid off with some degree of regularity, and old Hagan took a special pride and delight in erecting the General's "Wigwam," as he called it.[7] This was a large and commodious hospital tent, near the entrance of which Hagan had built a real brick chimney — none of your wooden affairs with barrel-tops — which was supplied throughout the whole winter with cords of the finest hickory wood. The inside was furnished with a plank floor, and a rough pine-board bedstead, on which the General's blankets and buffalo robe were spread, making a resting place scarcely less comfortable than the feathery couches of luxury and ease.

Our work, however, was interrupted toward the close of the month, most suddenly and unexpectedly. About the 25th or 26th of November, Genl. Meade commenced a movement against the right flank of our army, which has passed into history under the name of the "Mine Run Campaign." One of the General's scouts, coming in late at night, apprised us of the enemy's movement and in less time than it takes me to pen these lines, we were saddling our horses and moving out of camp. The night, I remember, was bitter cold — freezing hard — and it was as much as we could do to keep from grumbling at the unreasonable request of our Northern brethren who so unceremoniously demanded our presence at such an hour of the night and in such inclement weather. Our route lay near Gen. R.E. Lee's Headquarters, and Genl. Stuart paid him a short visit as we passed. Thence taking the road to Verdiersville we tramped along thro' the ice-crusted mud reaching that point a little before daybreak. The next day, or rather that morning, we pushed on down the plank road with a portion of Hampton's old brigade until we encountered the enemy's advance guard. Commencing the skirmish with them near Good Hope Church [New Hope Church], we drove them at first, but they retired to their infantry supports, and then bringing these up they forced us back a short distance. They seemed in no hurry to advance, and displayed only a small force of cavalry which soon retired behind their infantry skirmishers. Towards evening our infantry began to arrive, and Hampton's men, being relieved, were ordered to go into camp on the right of the road. Keeping up a good line of videttes along our whole front, Gen. Stuart retired for the night to a place near Verdiersville, immediately alongside the road, which had been selected that morning as our Hdqr. camp. Here we found the Hdqr. ambulance and wagon, and the General's faithful old servants Jake and Bob, and that princely cook of Major McClellan's[8] — old Albert; the camp-fire was blazing bright, the coffee steaming hot and the biscuits and fried middlin' waiting to be devoured. {Side Notation: alter} How long do you think it took to dismount, unsaddle and halter the horses, and gather 'round the fire? Warming our half-frozen limbs in the generous glow, and afterwards stretching out at full length on the soft pine-[word illegible] feeling that delightful sensation of repose which only the tired trooper knows how to enjoy. It was on such occa-

**MAJOR HENRY B. McCLELLAN,
ADJUTANT STUART'S STAFF**
*Courtesy of Williams College Archives
and Special Collections*

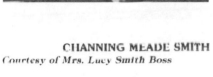

CHANNING MEADE SMITH
Courtesy of Mrs. Lucy Smith Boss

CAPTAIN WILLIAM M. McGREGOR
Courtesy of the Author

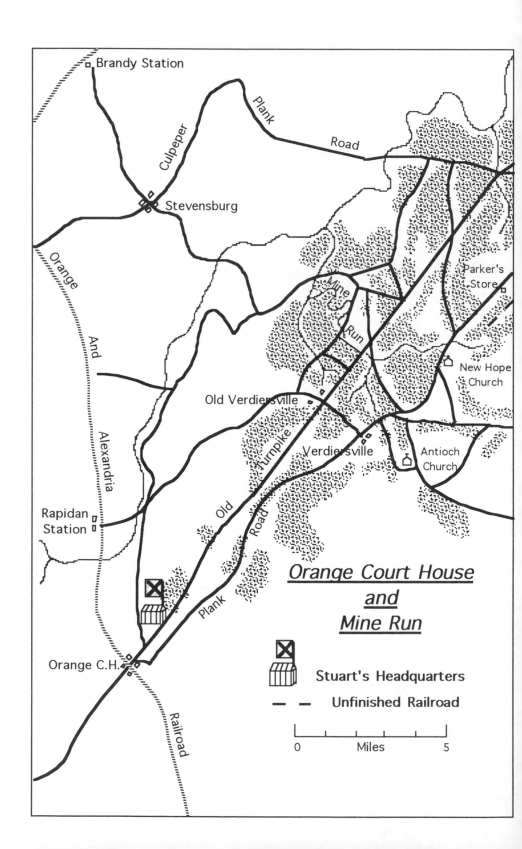

Brandy Station

Plank Road

Culpeper

Stevensburg

Orange

And

Alexandria

Rapidan Station

Orange C.H.

Plank Road

Railroad

Old Verdiersville

Old Turnpike

Verdiersville

Mine Run

Parker's Store

New Hope Church

Antioch Church

Orange Court House
and
Mine Run

Stuart's Headquarters

Unfinished Railroad

0   Miles   5

sions as these that Gen. Stuart showed himself in all the joyous qualities of his genial nature. The merry laugh, the hearty joke, the rousing chorus enlivened his camp-fire, and here he shone out as the Prince of Good Fellows with scarcely less brilliancy then when on the battle-field he claimed our willing tribute as Prince of Cavaliers.

Friday and Saturday, Nov. 27th and 28th, were spent in desultory skirmishing with the enemy's cavalry. A courier from Genl. [Brigadier General Thomas L.] Rosser arrived on Saturday evening with a dispatch from Genl. Rosser stating that Rosser had gotten into an ordnance train of the enemy's somewhere near the Brock Road, captured a large number of mules and burned the wagons. Channing Smith and Chewning brought the General a Headquarters flag which they had taken the night before on a visit to the tent of the General Comdg' the 5th Yankee Corps, and they gave us full information regarding the enemy's strength and position, having ridden through their columns on the march and visited their camps afterwards.[9]

On Sunday morning, Nov. 29th, bright and early, Genl. Stuart rode with his staff and escort over to the extreme right of our lines, then well established along the west side of the valley thro' which Mine Run flows, and after sending orders to Genl. Hampton to bring his division down the Catharpin Road, set out in that direction himself. I well remember the impatience with which he waited to learn that the command was on the way to join him, and how he sent courier after courier to hurry them up. The road was in bad order, muddy and slippery and the horses travelled with difficulty. What on earth was up? Where were we going? No man but Stuart knew. After marching probably 6 or 8 miles we left the Catharpin Road and struck off thro' some farms and woodland in the direction of the old railroad which was once intended to run from Fredericksburg to Orange Court House or Gordonsville. As we approached the line of this railroad, travelling a swampy difficult road thro' a thick body of woods, the sharp report of a pistol just in front rang out on the morning air, followed by the crack of a carbine and the whistle of a ball over our heads, causing us to straighten up in the saddles and unbuckle our holsters, for every man felt that we were in the presence of the enemy. In a few seconds, Chewning, the scout mentioned above, came galloping back and informed the General that he had fired at a picket standing on the railroad bank, who had returned his salute and then retreated. Gen. Stuart reproved him sharply for firing his pistol and rebuked him for not taking the man off his post without making such a row. But Chewning replied that he didn't feel exactly authorized to be so rude in view of the fact that there were three or four other Yankees with the first named gentleman, for he saw them all ride back together. Here we were then, nothing but the staff and escort of couriers, some 20 men in all, close upon the enemy's outposts. No time must be wasted or the whole effect of the surprise would be lost. What we were to do must

— 19 —

be done quickly. So without a minutes hesitation, Genl. Stuart turned to his staff and couriers and told us to Charge. "Here we go boys! The General's leading us. There's no getting out of this matter," — and away we went! Reaching the railroad embankment, we found it clear, but in the field beyond we could see the backs of the retreating pickets. Over we go, and raising a savage yell, our little column dashed gallantly across the field. Thunder and Mars! What is that I see standing in the Plank Road at Parker's Store? Cavalry, by the Powers! Yankee Cavalry, — in some confusion, it is true, but still enough to eat us all up at one mouthful! Bang! Bang! — the smoke rises all around them, and Whiz! Thud! there goes Archie's (my messmate's) horse down on his nose, and his rider playing leap-frog over his head. Zip! — a ball hits the pommel of my saddle, and I rein my horse in, somewhat doubtful of the success of this little affair. Some half a dozen of us halt about 75 yards from the Plank Road, and blaze away into the thick crowd of men and horses standing there, bringing down only two or three, that I could see, hardly enough to pay for our powder and ball. Whereas it seemed to me almost impossible to shoot into such a crowd without hitting something, and yet I ask any unprejudiced person or persons if it isn't a very difficult matter to hit the side of a barn if you are in momentary apprehension that the aforesaid barn is going to return the compliment.

Toler has gotten off a little to one side, on their flank, and is putting in some good shots. Channing Smith is firing right straight ahead and attracting their attention almost exclusively, for which I thank him with my whole heart, though I do feel really alarmed for him, and hope he won't be hit. Geo. Woodbridge is busy too.[10] I join Toler in the bushes on the left and after firing the only remaining load in my pistol, begin to think of leaving. Just then they break, and we advance to the road. In the bushes beyond is the camp of two regiments of Pennsylvania Cavalry, deserted and now in the hands of a half dozen of Stuart's couriers. Is it possible, I thought to myself, as I rode up to untie a splendid horse from the tree where his owner had left him, is it possible that those fellows are going to give up their camp without any more fighting than this? Before I could reach the horse, however, my question was fully answered. The clatter of horses' feet on the other side of the camp was heard, and in another second I saw them returning to the charge. I had scarcely time to turn my horse into the road and give him the spur, before they were back in the camp, and but for the intervention of a few friendly bushes, I would have been a prisoner. We retreated across the field back to the railroad bank; the time occupied in this little scrimmage could not have been more than 5 minutes in reality. It seemed to me, however, at least a half hour.

A squadron of the 7th Virginia Cavalry, Rosser's Brigade, now came up and went at them with a cheer. The enemy again broke and left in confusion. They surely must be gone now, thought we; not so. Again they had rallied, this time a short distance down the Plank Road, and back they came in gallant style, driving our squadron out of their camp. A portion of the 11th Regiment, Rosser's Brigade, then came forward and put an end to the affair, for a time, by a well directed charge, driving the enemy away. Then ensued a scene of disgraceful confusion. The men, attracted by the rich plunder of the camp, were scattered about picking up whatever they could find, and it was an utter impossibility to make them return to their ranks.

The enemy was not out of sight; indeed, they were in full view about 300 yards down the Plank Road, forming another squadron for a charge, which they seemed about to make, and receiving fresh accessions to their numbers from those who had escaped into the woods. Our men had crowded into the road in great disorder, and Generals Stuart, Rosser, and Gordon were endeavoring to reform them, or at any rate to get together an organized body in order to charge the enemy who were standing in the road below us. Rosser, with his clear and powerful voice and with great earnestness, was calling on his men to form in the road. He even implored them by an eloquent allusion to the lamented [Brigadier General Turner] Ashby, whose old regiment was then on the ground, to get back into their ranks and prepare to follow up their victory. It was all in vain. The disorder seemed only to increase; and yet the men seemed perfectly willing to do their duty, they only wanted to be told what do. It is easy enough for a commanding officer to cry, "Rally men! Form squadron!" etc. to a mixed crowd of cavalry just after a charge but how are you going to do it? The bugler, "most in general," ain't in hand — he's a priveleged [sic] character — or at least, he was with us, — the corporal or orderly sergeant may have been shot, or is out of the way, and where is the poor private, be he ever so willing to rally. It may be safely stated that the most difficult matter known in cavalry tactics is to reform a squadron after a successful charge.

So it was in this instance. But immediately upon Genl. Rosser's appeal to the memory of Ashby, a youth, a perfect boy, belonging to Co. B 11th Virginia Cavalry, galloped up to the color-bearer of his regiment, who was standing listlessly by, seized the colors, threw his bridle-rein down on his horse's neck, and raising the flag-staff with both hands high above his head, stuck spurs to his horse and dashed off alone towards the enemy.

The effect was instantaneous; such conspicuous gallantry was worth more than all the exhortations that could have been uttered, and as if with one impulse, the whole crowd of disordered horsemen spurred forward after their brave little leader straining every nerve in the sweeping charge to overtake him before he should have time to ride, defenseless and alone, into the midst of the dense, blue column standing steady to receive him. But not long did they so stand; the front files discharged shot after shot at him; nearer and nearer he approached, encouraged by our cheers and the sure hope of speedy support as we rapidly gained on him. In another instant I saw him poise the flag-staff, as a lance in rest; the blue squadron wavers, a few break off from the rear, and the flash of two or three pistols, close up behind our flag-bearer, hastens the determination of the rest. They wheel, they fly, and I saw our colors dipped, with the violence of a heavy blow, across the yellow seamed back and shoulders of a retreating Yankee. On we went, and for three miles a regular fox-chase was kept up, passing every now and then some poor mortally wounded "blue-devil," lying in the muddy road. {Side notation: But our only thought, in the excitement of the chase, was "Let us score their backs, And scratch 'em up, as we take hares behind; 'Tis sport to maul a runner."}[11]

About twenty were captured and sent back towards Parker's Store. The rest having made good their escape, we called off the pursuit, report having been brought in of another camp of the enemy near Chancellorsville, which was only a mile in our front. When our men assembled there were nearly two hundred, members of every regiment in Rosser's Brigade. Col. [Colonel Thomas] Marshall of the 7th was found to be the ranking officer and requested to take command. So we walked our horses slowly back, laughing and talking over the many amusing scenes and incidents of the pursuit; this man's horse had fallen with him and sent him head foremost into a mudhole, the same thing had happened to two or three of the prisoners, and pretty looking objects they were — while one of the men told me he had ridden up alongside a Yankee Captain and presenting his pistol (which, by the way, was _empty_) ordered him to surrender. The Captain refused; the man insisted, threatening instant death, etc., till finally there was nothing else to do but club his pistol and knock the Captain out of his saddle.

I remember just here, meeting Captain Hugh McGuire, (afterward killed on the retreat) of the 11th Regiment, and shaking hands with him, his handsome face glowing with pleasant excitement, and his bright eye beaming kindness, as he greeted me with cheerful smile and cordial grasp, proof of a friendship formed in our school-boy days.[12] We rode along side by side. And now, what follows must be told briefly. The fortune of war is more fickle perhaps than that of any other phase of human experience. We had hardly set out on our return to the main body of our command, which, from the sound of the guns, seemed to have commenced a fresh engagement at Parker's Store, when a trooper galloped up to Col. Marshall and informed him that a full regiment of Yankee cavalry were coming around the bend of the road at a charge and were at that time only a few hundred yards from us. They had recaptured all the prisoners sent back by us and were now bearing down to gobble us up. This intelligence, you may imagine, was astonishing and alarming. Nearly every one of us had emptied his pistol, and we were too much exhausted to think of meeting a charge with our sabres, many of us being without them. Everybody knows that there's no such thing as getting _off_ the Plank Road in that part of the Spotsylvania Wilderness. Looking around us we could see nothing but the thick undergrowth of black-jacks and willow-oaks, standing on each side, as secure as a stone wall, in their knotty impenetrability. There seemed then no retreat, for an enemy's camp was in our rear, alarmed by the fugitives we had just chased into it, and in front was a regiment, with drawn sabres, in close order — columns of fours — coming at full speed to make short work of us. The prospect was unusually blue. No amount of military genius could avail anything at such a juncture, courage wasn't lacking, nobody seemed very much alarmed, but what was to be done? Col. Marshall sat at the head of the column, looking calmly up the road. The men at the rear didn't even know why we had halted, and accordingly closed the column up tight, blocking up the road entirely. Col. Marshall's horse was pushed a little way off the road to one side, where there was sort of a hogwallow and a path from it leading into the bushes. Oh! fortunate accident, the only thing that could have saved the entire command from capture or complete rout. The colonel's horse stepped into the path, wide enough to admit one at a time, and ordering us to follow him we pressed into the bushes one by one. But before half of the column had gotten out of the road, the enemy appeared. Seeing us moving and thinking, no doubt, that we were deploying for a skirmish, they hesitated. Those of us who had any loads left in our pistols let drive at them. They returned the shots, and a little fusillade was kept up for a minute or two. But the head of our column had struck an old worn out road running a short distance from the Plank Road and parallel to it and then bending off to the South, and into this we turned, struck a trot, and showed the enemy as clean a pair of heels as the condition of the roads would allow. I don't think we lost a man in this whole affair, except the guard with the recaptured prisoners. In a long and roundabout march of several hours, we made our way back to the scene of the morning's encounter, arriving there just in time to join the rear guard of the command which had been fighting there all day, and now at dusk was leaving to return to our lines on Mine Run. The reader must understand that we had been all day long in the rear of Meade's Army, Parker's Store being only a few miles, say 3 or 4, from where his line of battle was then established.

The march back to Mine Run was a difficult one. Shortly after leaving the battle-field, it turned very cold — freezing cold, — and the night was unusually dark. On we trudged, — halting every now and then to let the column close up, — scattered by having to cross so many bogs and swamps. About 2 o'clock A.M. we went into camp, — not a soul of us knowing where we were or how we had gotten there. I was still with Hugh McGuire, and we lay down together by a tremendous fire of rails which his men had built, regardless of the stringent orders not to burn the fences.

I woke at sunrise, and saddling my horse, started to find my General, from whom I had been separated ever since that charge down the Plk Road. It was a glorious day, — biting cold, but clear as a bell. Looking away across the country, I could see heavy columns of the enemy's infantry, the early sunlight glancing from their bayonets, as they filed continuously around a point of pine woods about two miles distant. I soon found General Stuart and gave him an account of myself, which proving satisfactory, he sent me to Genl. [Major General Cadmus M.] Wilcox, whose Division occupied the right of our line, with orders to remain there until the attack of the enemy, now expected every hour, should begin, (The road to Wilcox's Hdqrs. ran immediately in rear & some twenty yards from our breastworks) and report to him (Genl. Stuart) from time to time how the fight progressed. Fortunately for me, no attack was made that day; — if there had been I think it more than probable that I would never have witnessed another, or even seen much of that. As I rode along the line of Wilcox's Division, I could but be struck with the evident look of satisfaction with which his men seemed to regard their breastworks, and I venture to say that there were few men in those ranks who would not have welcomed any attack that the enemy could make upon them.

The 1st of December, clear and cold, passed away quietly, with scarcely a shot fired along the skirmish line. The enemy spent the day in strengthening their breastworks, and we were occupied in doing the same in ours. The 2nd, and perhaps the 3rd, for I do not distinctly remember, was spent in this way, the troops sleeping on their arms all night, and manning the works at early dawn in eager expectation of a general engagement. Every evening at dark, General Stuart would leave the lines, and ride slowly back in our camp among the old pines not far from Verdiersville. Here we would gather 'round the campfire, piled high with blazing pine logs, and after drinking as much of Albert's good coffee as each of us could get, and eating our "hard-tack" and bacon, the pipes were lit, and we smoked and talked ourselves to sleep. To this luxury, however, General Stuart was an entire stranger, — never in the whole course of his life having used tobacco in any shape; nor did he ever, until he received his mortal wound, drink a drop of an intoxicating liquor. His splendid physique needed no such stimulant to action, and his extraordinary powers of endurance were the result of a life absolutely free from intemperance or excess.

On the third or fourth day after the enemy had established themselves in our front, it became evident that they had no intention of attacking us. Accordingly, the rumor was circulated that we were about to assume the offensive. I cannot here state positively whether such was the intention of General Lee, but I remember that the impression very strongly prevailed that we were going to make the attack. On the morning of the 5th of December (I think; — maybe it was the 4th) it was discovered that the works in our front were empty.[13] Not a Yankee was to be seen. Pushing forward in the direction of the Rappahannock River, Genl. Stuart with one brigade of cavalry came upon their rear-guard just as they were crossing over to the Culpeper side. The ford was too well guarded to admit of his attacking them; he sent me back with a message to Gen. Lee to this effect. I found Genl. Lee at Parker's Store, together with Genl. [Lieutenant General] A.P. Hill, the head of whose column had reached that point in pursuit of the enemy. Delivering my message to Gen. Lee, the troops were at once ordered back, and thus ended the Mine Run Campaign.

I shall never forget the wild enthusiasm of those men of Hill's Corps, as they cheered Marse Robert [General Robert E. Lee], who with his Staff & Escort, passed along the front of a whole Division. The men had been halted in the road, and were lying down to rest. As they saw General Lee coming they would rise, form & dress their ranks, and when he passed they rent the very atmosphere with deafening hurrahs.

I leave it for the historians of the war, and other military critics, to comment on this movement of Genl. Meade's. To the rank and file of Our Army, however, it seemed a clear case of "back down." After crossing the Rappahannock River with his whole Army — not a shot being fired to prevent it — he selected the position for his line of battle in front of the only two Corps of the Army of Northern Virginia, — numbering scarcely one third of his force, — and there entrenched himself in the heaviest field-works that any army ever made, — afraid to make the attack himself and fearful lest it should be made upon him. And when this fear had amounted to conviction, he withdrew under the cover of darkness, with a haste which certainly excited our surprise, if it did not command our admiration.

Our wonder is immeasurably increased when we reflect that this was the first time since the disastrous battle of Gettysburg that the two armies had been drawn up face to face. The whole North had been assured by the Press, the Pulpit and the Cabinet that the Rebellion was suppressed, — the Rebel Army demoralized, starving and only waiting to ground their arms in the mud and mire of the "last ditch." But here, at Mine Run, the Army of Northern Virginia, weakened by the absence of [Lieutenant General James] Longstreet's Corps, had nevertheless boldly advanced to meet the issue of battle which Gen. Meade thus forced upon them. The retention of Gen. Meade in command of the Federal Army, even for the short time which elapsed before he yielded it to Gen. [Lieutenant General Ulysses S.] Grant, was the strongest and most flattering proof of the estimation in which his high military abilities were held by the Washington Government. No other man in the Yankee Nation could have thus afforded to brave the fury of a disappointed Public without being prepared to suffer the decapitation which had invariably been visited upon his blundering predecessors.

———

Winter had set in with more than usual severity when the troops returned to their old camps around Orange Court House, and along the Rapidan. A great part of the Cavalry had been disbanded and been sent home to procure fresh horses even before the Mine Run Campaign began, — and now this absolutely necessary process to fill up our ranks was continued by Gen. Stuart. The system of "Horse Details" was greatly enlarged, and every effort was made to organize more efficiently and equip more thoroughly our still badly provided Cavalry Corps. I may be pardoned here for saying a word in praise of that noble Corps, which for such a long period of the war had received nothing but curses and abuse from our bretheren [sic] of the Infantry and Artillery. The close of the year 1863 witnessed a considerable change of sentiment in this respect among the men of the Bayonet and the Bomb. The Bristoe Campaign had opened their eyes to the fact that the Cavalry did really do some work after all. The credit they bestowed upon us then, — and I assert it without the slightest fear of contradiction — would have been awarded all along, if they had been, — as they then were, — actual witnesses of our work. During that campaign, the Cavalry operated close to, and many times in the presence of the Infantry, without their being engaged at all; — and indeed, the only successes our Army gained on that trip, were obtained by our Corps.

Cavalry has well been styled the "Eyes and Ears" of an Army; the other two Arms, to use a paradoxical expression, may be termed the "hands and feet;" and it would have been vastly better if these latter members of that glorious body — the Army of Northern Virginia — had recognized & appreciated, a little earlier in the struggle, the true philosophy contained in those simple verses of Holy Writ: "If the foot shall say: Because I am not the hand, I am not of the body; is it therefore not of the body." "And the eye cannot say unto the hand, I have no need of thee: nor again the head to the feet, I have no need of you." (I Corinthians XII, 15. 21.)

But without stopping to consider what advantages might have accrued to the service from the harmony and good will which these moral reflections might have established and strengthened. I proceed to relate something of our life at Camp "Wigwam," as Gen. Stuart called it, during the winter of '63-'64.

Immediately on our return to the old camp, the waste places were rebuilt, the wooden chimneys were daubed afresh with the red mud of old Orange, the wall-tents were again pitched in front of them, and we settled down for the winter. And here memory fails me in the effort to recall, in the order of their occurrence, the events of our daily life. I look back along the dreary lapse of seven years, and the days and months of winter which then seemed an interminable age, now appear at the end of the dim vista as the faint semblance of a pleasant dream. Dull days would come; it was impossible to escape them; Rain, Sleet and Snow make camp-life almost unbearable; but with the return of sunshine our spirits would rise, and Stuart's Headquarters were not wanting in men or means to drive away ennui.

Music, Song and laughter were the natural allies of our beloved Commander. It was in this camp that one of the members of the Staff, Capt. Wm.

W. Blackford, composed that stirring song "The Cavalier's Glee," and our Glee-Club, which could boast quite a number of good voices, here first woke the echoes with the bold notes of that grand old Chorus.[14] I transcribe the song from memory:

"The Cavalier's Glee"

Spur on! Spur on! We love the bounding
Of barbs that bear us to the fray,
"The Charge" our bugles now are sounding,
And our bold Stuart leads the way!
    The path of honor lies before us,
    Our hated foemen gather fast.
    At home bright eyes are sparkling for us,
    We will defend them to the last.

Spur on! Spur on! We love the rushing
Of steeds that spurn the turf they tread,
We'll thro' the Northern ranks go rushing,
With our proud battleflag o'er head.

Chorus:

Spur on! Spur on! we love the flashing
Of blades that struggle to be free,
'Tis for our sunny South they're clashing;
For Household, God and Liberty.

Chorus:[15]

I have already given a brief description of this camp — "Wigwam" — as it was called by General Stuart, in memory perhaps of some of his camps in the far West, during the time when he was on the warpath against hostile Indians. I may as well, however, refresh the reader's memory with a fuller sketch as our sojourn here was probably of greater length than in any previous winter quarters, extending from about the 1st of Nov. 1863, to the 4th of May 1864. About one mile and a half northeast of Orange Court House, in a narrow valley thickly studded with pine and cedar trees, our tents were pitched; there was some regularity in the manner of laying off the encampment, a feature seldom found in any of the Corps, Division, or Brigade Headquarters of the Army of Northern Virginia. As you entered the valley from the direction of Orange Court House, the road from which wound through the open, rolling fields belonging to the estate of Mr. Scott, you passed first, on the left, the camp and tents of Genl Stuart's escort of couriers, commanded by Lieut. Hagan, a veteran who deserves honorable mention in these memoirs. Near this group of tents was the Forage-Sergt's quarters, easily distinguished by the two large

CAPTAIN CHARLES GRATTAN, ORDNANCE OFFICER STUART'S STAFF

Courtesy of
George Grattan Weston

JOHN B. FONTAINE, STUART'S STAFF SURGEON

Courtesy of
The Valentine Museum
Richmond, Virginia

stacks of hay and the piles of corn, with which Sergt Buckner kept us so well supplied during this long and severe winter. Here too was the tent of Sergt Ben Weller, the ante-bellum owner of the <u>Woolly-Horse;</u> he was also one of General Stuart's best and most reliable couriers; active, brave, keen-witted, and a good judge of horse-flesh; indeed, he supplied the General with one of the best horses that ever was brought to the Army — a powerful iron-grey, the horse, by the way, on which the Genl was mounted when he received his mortal wound near Yellow Tavern.[16] Following the road a hundred yards further on, the first tent on the left was Major McClellan's, our Adjutant General, next to that and about 30 feet distant was Major Venable's, and then at about the same interval came the General's tent, a splendid specimen of canvass, beautifully pitched near an immense pine tree, having a brick chimney, a plank floor, a frame-door swing on hinges, in short, the most comfortable looking tent, inside and out, that I ever saw in any camp.[17] Along in front of these three tents ran a saw-dust walk, terminating just beyond the Adjutant General's tent at the door of a log-hut, which had been built for Major McClellan's clerks. Behind this row of tents and about 20 yards further up the slope were three other tents pitched at the same intervals of distance from each other, and approached by saw-dust walks from the main walk. These tents were occupied by the remaining members of the staff: Capt. Charles Grattan, Ordnance Officer, Capt. John Esten Cooke, Assistant Adjutant General, and Dr. John B. Fontaine, Medical Director of the Cavalry Corps.[18] To the left and in front of Gen. Stuart's tent, and almost in the bottom of the valley, was a solitary tent-fly, raised about three feet from the ground, and under which stood our mess table, a permanent structure, made of pine boards and set off with rude benches — chestnut logs split in two and hewed down to some degree of smoothness. A little further down the valley, during a portion of the early winter stood the tent of Lieut. Col. [Lieutenant Colonel George] St. Leger Grenfell, who occupied for a short time the position of Inspector Genl of the Cavalry Corps. This officer had come to Gen. Stuart from the Western Army, and was assigned to this duty by the War Dept. at Richmond. He was a curious compound of soldierly qualities and personal idiosyncrasies; at times, he would talk with officers & couriers in a sort of general harangue, relating some of the most wonderful anecdotes that were ever heard, and again, he would avoid all society confining himself closely to his tent, in company with his big yellow Bull-dog, and appearing only at meals, or at work on his two magnificent horses with curry comb and brush, allowing no other groom to touch their velvet coats. He disappeared from our midst about X-mas, 1863, and I heard of him no more until his arrest somewhere in the North, by the Yankee Gov't, charged with an attempt to burn Chicago, (which event was only postponed a few years later) {Side notation: Oct. 9, 1871} tried and convicted, and sentenced to spend the remainder of his days on the arid sands of the Dry Tortugas. Already he was well stricken in years, being upwards of sixty. A rumor has been set afloat since the war that he was drowned in attempting to escape by swimming from his place of confinement. The story of his life would doubtless be one of thrilling interest, for he seemed to have tried every phase of human existence in every quarter of the globe; and if he has any relative or friend in England, or comrade in the British Army, of which he claimed to be an officer, it would gratify the curiosity of many survivors of the Army of Northern Virginia to hear something more about him.[19]

I have been led into this digression by an irresistible impulse of memory, and I fear I shall have to ask pardon for many more such departures from the strict line of my story. It is only when in actual campaigning that it becomes necessary to preserve the order of time, and I have already given fair warning that the reader may expect to be interrupted here and there with the account of matters, sketches of persons and events, that will detain him, it is hoped not unpleasantly, from the stirring scenes which are soon to follow.

"Camp Wigwam" then must be kept before the mind's eye, if the patient reader wishes to see more of the daily life of Gen. Stuart and his military family, and to understand fully their situation. On the hill in front of us, looking towards Orange Court House a brigade of Infantry of Hill's Corps was encamped for about a month, but moved its quarters after consuming all the firewood in their reach, and stealing some few of the cooking utensils of our couriers. The interval between the date of our return from Mine Run and the "Christmas holidays" was spent in making everything as comfortable as possible. Being a courier at the time myself, I speak from vivid recollection of having to cut and bring wood, mix mud and daub tent chimneys and do many odd jobs of a like character. Our mess, which consisted of Pegram, Berkeley and Grant, sometimes lived "high" on beef and potatoes or hard-tack and middlin', as the case might be, — and at other times nearly starved on account of sheer laziness or disgust at having to cook for ourselves. Berkeley had a negro-boy who sometimes cooked for us and sometimes he didn't. Christmas came and found us all in low spirits at the prospect of a dull time. At night we would often get together our Amateur Glee-Club with old Sam Sweeney as leader of the band, Bob, his cousin, the lefthanded violinist, Pegram with his flute, and occasionally Major McClellan with his fine guitar, and your humble servant with the triangle and all assembling in the General's tent, go through with a mixed program of songs, jokes, back-stepping and fun-making generally until the general, tiring of our performances, would rise up on his buffalo-robe and say, "Well, Good evening to you all, gentlemen," and in five minutes thereafter the camp would be hushed in sleep.[20]

On Xmas night, 1863, a serenading party left camp to go into the Court House, and give the ladies some music. How well I remember Sam Sweeney's banjo that night!, — almost the last time he ever played it, poor fellow, —

for in less than two weeks from that night he was in his grave. Von Borcke in his "Memoirs of the Confederate War" has, unintentionally I am sure, done Sam an injustice, — or in other words he has mistaken <u>Sam</u> for his cousin <u>Bob</u>.[21] Both of them were excellent musicians, but Sam Sweeney was the world-renowned banjo-player, while Bob Sweeney's instrument was the violin. They were both "good fellows," — and richly deserve the praise which Capt. John Esten Cooke has bestowed upon their personal and artistic merits. They were both with us that night serenading; — stopping at one house to awake, as we thought, the fair sleepers with our dulcet strains, we found that they had not retired, and as soon as they discovered who we were, the door was thrown open and all hands invited to enter. We accepted, and found in the parlor an egg-nogg party going on. It was at once proposed to clear the floor for a dance, and in a few minutes our partners were selected, the music struck up, and we chased the golden hours with flying feet until the dawn of the day reminded us of our camp behind the hills, towards which with unwilling steps we wound our way, first having escorted our ladies to their respective homes, thus realizing the sentiment of the old Sailor's song —

> "We'll dance all night, till broad day light
> And go home with the girls in the morning."

Thus the days and nights of winter passed away. My position as a courier, of course, debarred me in great measure from the society and intercourse of the Staff officers, tho' I will say that there were few of Genl. Stuart's staff who made distinction between the starred, barred & gold-laced [paper torn; at least one word missing] the collar-less, cravat-less, dirty-jacketed high-p [paper torn; at least one word missing] the said private behaved himself like a gentleman [paper torn; a word possibly missing].

It was not long, however, after the Xmas frolic before I was called upon to change my mess, in a manner as gratifying as it was unexpected. I had retired for the night, or in soldier's phrase, "turned in" to my bunk in Maj. McClellan's tent and was peacefully dreaming, when I felt a heavy hand on my shoulder and turning over recognized Major Venable, who had waked me, saying "get up, General Stuart wants to see you in his tent." It didn't take me more than a minute to complete my toilet, which consisted of pulling on a heavy pair of cavalry boots and slipping on my jacket, and rubbing my drowsy eyes, I groped my way to the General's tent. Knocking at the door I was told to "Come in," and entered finding the General stretched out on his couch with Venable sitting near him. I wondered what was coming, and thought some trick or joke was about to be played on me by my laughter-loving chief; for I had fancied I could detect a suppressed smile on Maj. Venable's countenance. Pointing to his open desk, on which the General's private letter book was lying, with pens, ink, and paper, he very quietly said, "Sit down there, Garnett, and copy that letter for me." I did as I was told, and taking up a pen, not even yet fully awake, commenced to write, as follows.:

"Headquarters Cavalry Corps
Army of Nor 'n Va
January 27, 1864

Gen. S. Cooper, A&I Genl.
Richmond.
General,

I have the honor to recommend Private Theodore S. Garnett, Jr., of Co. "F" 9th Va Cav, for appointment as 1st Lieut. and Aide-de-Camp, to be assigned to duty on my Staff, vice Lieut. Chiswell Dabney promoted."[22]

Before finishing that sentence, I rose from my seat, blushing like a girl, and stammered out my thanks to General Stuart, grasping his strong hand in both of mine and pledging him my life-long gratitude and service. He burst into the heartiest laughter and seemed to enjoy hugely my utter surprise and confusion. Major Venable, joining in with his powerful lungs, and thus making it "worse confounded." I finished the letter to Gen. Cooper and after a short conversation with the Genl went back to my blankets, but not to sleep, for my heart was thumping away and every pulse throbbing with pleasure and pride, at this the first mark of that great soldier's esteem for me, a pleasure and pride which I can never again experience, and for which I would not exchange now any memory of my life.

The next morning, the 28th of January, I was invited to breakfast with General Stuart, and received the congratulations of my brethren of the Staff.

Not many days after this, Gen. Stuart told me to get myself ready to pay a flying visit with him to Richmond. He made me ride over to General R.E. Lee's Headquarters, about two miles distant from ours, and get his three days leave-of-absence approved. This, by the way, was, I think the first and only leave-of-absence ever applied for by Gen. Stuart. No man in the army was ever more closely and continuously at his Post than he. When the necessary papers had been approved by General Lee, we started for the Depot at Orange Court House and were soon on our journey. At Gordonsville we changed cars, getting on board the train from Staunton, I was fortunate enough to find in the ladies' car a fair young friend Miss J.C. from Winchester who was travelling with her brother to Richmond. He gave me his seat beside her and we were soon engaged in a lively and to me very agreeable conversation. The train had been in motion about a half an hour, when I told her I wanted to introduce General Stuart to her. She hesitated and finally declined, saying that

HEROS VON BORCKE, INSPECTOR, STUART'S STAFF

Courtesy of Mrs. Adele Mitchell

LIEUTENANT CHISWELL DABNEY, AIDE-DE-CAMP STUART'S STAFF
Courtesy of The Pittsylvania Historical Society

she had heard that the General never failed to kiss all the young ladies he met. I begged her not to be alarmed; that I would apply to him for her "exemption-papers," and then I had to tell her seriously that these reports about the General's kissing propensities were slanderously exaggerated; that it was true, I had seen him surrounded by a bevy of beautiful young ladies, who submitted most gracefully, nay ever cheerfully, to the trying ordeal of a kiss from General Stuart, and that too, in the open street of a Virginia village, when the smoke and dim of battle had scarcely subsided around them; that I had never known him, in cold blood, and no firing going on, to demand any unwilling tribute of the sort. She persisted in her refusal, much to my regret, for I could catch the General's eye every now and then, and see that he was thinking me wonderfully remiss, and I didn't feel at liberty then, as I did afterwards on one occasion when he was running me about it, to tell him the cause of my failure to give him an introduction.

Our visit to Richmond was a pleasant one. Having many friends there, it was always a pleasure to me to find myself within its hospitable walls. At this season, the city was filled with strangers, as indeed it was during the whole war; but especially cheerful did everything look, and I rec'd several invitations to "Starvation parties" (falsely so called) whereat the youth and beauty of Richmond's fairest and best were want to assemble, and even in the midst of war revive the scenes of Peace. But our three days sped away so quickly to admit of such indulgences, and we returned promptly to camp when our leave was out.

I had employed my time in making considerable changes in my wardrobe and made arrangements to purchase another horse. After the loss of my horses in Maryland I had been riding a most miserable Yankee "cob," and General Stuart's first instruction to me was "Go get another horse, and to keep well-mounted."[23] I accordingly purchased a handsome black mare from General Stuart named "Lily of the Valley," for the sum of $1500, tho' I settled the debt with $1200 of New Issue Confederate Notes. She was a beautiful animal, tho' having too much life and spirit at that time for cavalry service. She had carried Gen. Stuart on many a long march, but I don't think she was ever much of a favorite with him. I must stop here to say a word about Stuart's horses. He had with him, when we entered this camp, these horses, "Virginia," "Maryland," and "Star of the East." "Virginia" was a magnificent bay mare, splendidly formed and carried her rider as easily as a rocking chair. When I last saw her, the weather had been just cold enough to put the velvet on her coat and she was the most perfect specimen of equine beauty on which my eyes had ever rested. "Maryland" was a bay horse smaller in size than "Virginia," and more compactly made. Strong, sinewy and active, knowing what hard work was and able and willing to do it. He had been presented to General Stuart by a patriotic citizen of Maryland whose house we passed on one of our raids into that state. "Star of the East," or "Star," as he was usually called, was a sorrel horse, with light mane and tail, and the veteran of the whole stud, having carried Gen. Stuart from the very beginning of the war. All three of these horses died in this camp. They were attacked with the terrible disease called "Glanders" and sunk away one after the other, Maryland being the last to die. Strange to say none of the other horses were affected by the disease. It was after the death of these, his favorite steeds, that Gen. Stuart purchased from Ben Weller the heavy iron grey on whose back he rec'd his mortal wound. He had, however, brought into camp a young horse which he used to call his "pony," presented to him by a gentleman living in Louisa County, and it was with these two horses that he commenced the Campaign of 1864.[24]

It may be that my reader is by this time somewhat impatient for the campaign of '64 to begin. Not so however were we. There are two or three little "scrimmages" to be described before the campaign opens. Besides, what shall I say of the kind friends we made in and around Orange Court House? Can I ever forget Mrs. B's hospitable manner. To her, and to her fair daughter we were indebted for many, many charming evenings. It was an event of almost weekly occurrence to get together our string-band and drive over to the village and set everybody in that house to dancing.

On special occasions the General would accompany us, but most frequently he left us to our own devices, and our party usually consisted of Major Venable, Dr. Fontaine, Willie Pegram, Lieut. Webb and any guest or friend who happened to be staying with us.[25] And here I am reminded * {* — reference to side notation: [first line partially illegible] There were balls in camp in some of the dark times of the Revolution. "We had a little dance at my quarters," writes Genl Greene from Middlebrook in March 1779. "His Excellence and Mrs. Greene danced upward of three hours without once sitting down. Upon the whole we had a pretty little frisk."}

(Feb. 6, 1872. In reading today, I came across a song written by J. Hamilton Reynolds and sung by W. Balfe at a dinner given to Chas. Kemble by the Garrick Club, Jan. 10, 1837. One verse of which I will here transcribe as follows:

"Let the curtain come down! Let the scene pass away.
There's an autumn when summer hath lavished its day;
we may sit by the fire, when we can't by the lamp,
And repeople the banquet, — re-soldier the camp.
Oh! nothing can rob us of memory's gold,
And tho' he quits the gorgeous, and we may grow old,
with our Shakespeare at heart, and bright forms in our brain
we can dream up our Siddons and Kembles again.
    Well! wealthy we have been, tho' fortune may frown
    And they cannot but say we have had the crown."

This verse might be paraphrased and made a beautiful tribute to the noble dead — Jackson and Stuart.)

The reader must however, draw on his imagination for an account of these visits, and fancy himself in our situation before he can appreciate the pleasure they gave us. He can easily see tho', that in the long time of our stay around Orange Court House we must have formed friends, and some of us even stronger attachments among its hospitable matrons and fascinating maidens. It is therefore a natural desire the writer has to put on record here his gratitude as a soldier and his respect as a citizen for the kindness and hospitality received at the hands of the good people of Orange during the winter of '64.

Not far from our camp, but on the other side of the Rapidan River, lived our friend Dr. G. and his accomplished and beautiful wife (Miss G.B. that was). She had been my friend in her girlhood, and it was a pleasure to find her, tho' surrounded by nearly half a dozen splendid children, as young and bright as in the days when she graced her noble old homestead at Baybrook. In the early part of the winter, our visits to Dr. G's were frequent, and the General, accompanied by nearly his whole staff, with the two Sweeneys bringing up the rear, would ride over the river by moon-light, and tho' it was outside the picket line, make Dr. G's house his temporary Headquarters. If any of our party are still alive I wonder if they remember taking part in a game we played one evening called the "Prussian Ambuscade." I remember with almost equal pleasure a basket of sausages and cake which Mrs. G. sent me at Xmas, rejoicing the heart of every member of my mess.

The winter was dragging its weary length away, the snow and mud keeping both armies quiet, and save the occasional return of some of our scouts, or a visit from Major [John Singleton] Mosby, we had little or nothing to remind us of our Northern brethren.[26] Now and then a prisoner or deserter would arrive, and as quietly disappear in the direction of the Libby, or that other place which the Confederate Gov't kept for the accommodation of all first-class deserters who wished to return to private life in their Northern homes by means of the underground railroad. This was an institution surrounded by such mystery that no Confederate soldier to my knowledge ever discovered either of its termini. It was the opinion of many soldiers in the field that it was a consummate humbug, offering a premium to spies, and making that usually hazardous employment perfectly free from danger. It's professed object was to increase the desertions from the Yank Army by promising deserters safe and speedy transit to their homes in the North. Notices to this effect were published in English, French and German & circulated energetically across the picket-line

A novel case of desertion came under my notice when in this camp. One day a youthful looking couple, the one a Yankee soldier, the other a Virginia girl, came riding into camp under the escort of one man from the outpost.

They gave Genl. Stuart an account of themselves pretty much as follows; In answer to a question from the Genl. as to the Yankee's pedigree, he replied, "I am of Irish consent," and then proceeded to say that he had 'listed in the Yankee Army for want of something better to do, and had met his present companion — the young girl — at her home near the camp of his regiment in Culpeper. He made love to her, and was happy to say that she reciprocated his affection, and agreed to marry him on condition of his deserting at once and going with her into the Confederacy. He didn't even think twice about it, so glad was he to come to terms with her. So he stole two horses from his regiment one night and here they were, looking for a preacher to tie the knot, which they both wanted done as quickly as the nature of the case and "the exigencies of the service" would permit. They were accordingly sent on to the Court House without delay, tho' one of the couriers remarked as they passed out of camp, "That gal must ha' wanted a husband the very worst sort!"

Occasionally the monotony of camp-life would be varied by the arrival of Burke, or Stringfellow, or Toler, or Curtis, scouts who spent most of their time inside the enemy's lines and making their appearance only when important movements were about to begin, or changes in the military position made it necessary for them to "come out" and report to General Stuart.[27] It was this tried and trusty body of scouts to which Gen. Stuart owed much of his success in war. No commander was ever served more faithfully than these men served Stuart. No movement of troops, not a re-enforcement was ever received, nor an encampment changed in Gen. Meade's Army that was not speedily reported at our Headquarters, and the information at once forwarded to Gen. R.E. Lee. It was this in a great measure that made Gen. Stuart of such inestimable service to our Great [word illegible].

The Cavalry Corps, (for the Division had, during [at least two words illegible] of '63 been divided into two, one under Maj. Gen. Hampton and the other under Maj. Gen. Fitz Lee) as has already been stated, was well-nigh disbanded at this time. The only cavalry that Stuart kept with him around Orange Court House was one small brigade commanded by Brig. Gen. [Brigadier General Lunsford L.] Lomax, which was camped near Barnett's Ford on the Rapidan. Gordon's Brigade of Hampton's Division was at Guiney's Station forty miles distant from us on the Richmond Fredericksburg and Potomac Railroad — while the remnants of Wickham's & [Brigadier General John R.] Chambliss' Brigades were in camp near Charlottesville, where also was the camp of [Captain James] Breathed's Battalion of Horse Artillery.[28] Rosser's Brigade was somewhere near Lexington and rapidly filling up with the hardy mountaineers who prided themselves on being members of the "Laurel Brigade," each one of them having the lappel [sic] of his jacket decorated with a green leaf stitched on perhaps by wife, mother or sweetheart. The cavalry camp at Charlottesville was broken up early in the winter, the men going to their homes for fresh horses.

In the midst of this lazy, quiet life, we were all startled early one morning in February by a report brought in by one of our scouts that the Yankee Cavalry were moving towards our left. Hastily mounting his horse Gen. Stuart started at once towards Barnett's ford with only one or two couriers, Ellis and Weller, or Brofford and Freed, (or Goode and George) I forget which, who happened to have their horses saddled at the time, leaving instructions for his staff to follow him immediately.[29] I soon found him in company with Gen. Lomax giving instructions as to posting a battery which had just reached the heights overlooking the Ford; he was sitting quietly on his horse and directing his field-glasses towards the woods on the opposite side of the river whence the long lines of blue cavalry were emerging at a walk. In the field on their side, a heavy skirmish line of dismounted troopers was deployed, and now and then a stray shot from their carbines would whistle musically over our heads. On our side of the river and close down to the Ford was a strong line of rifle-pits which was well-filled with a brigade of infantry, [Brigadier General James H.] Lane's Brigade of A.P. Hill's Corps, and on their left we understood there was still another brigade of Infantry. This encouraging state of things, added to the magnificent defensive position we held, gave us all a feeling of such perfect security, that we began to pray for an attack to be made right in front. It was a beautiful scene, the clear sunlight bathed the landscape in a golden flood, and glanced in dazzling splendor from the burnished sabres of the hostile squadrons in the plain below us. A rattling fire runs along the skirmish lines, which suddenly ceases as the announcement is made that the enemy are preparing to charge. From my position near the battery on the hill-side, I saw the first squadron that led off; gallantly and in beautiful order they strike a gallop, and I wondered what fool could have ordered such a charge, across a swollen stream, at a rocky ford, and in the face of two brigades of infantry lying within fifty feet of the water's edge. But on they come, tho' hidden now from the view of our men by a slight rise of the river bank, over which however they must soon appear if they keep up that gait. Suddenly the leading files burst over the crest in full view of our whole line, and not 200 yards off, but imagine our surprise and indignation, when with one impulse and with a noise like the explosion of a powder-magazine, every musket is discharged at these half-dozen horsemen, not one of whom is touched, and the whole volley flies harmlessly over the heads of their comrades. Had that fire been reserved for 15 seconds of time, not one of that Yankee squadron could have survived that charge. As it was they wheeled quickly under cover of the embankment and escaped. If any of our Northern brethren should read this account who were in the charge, let them reflect that they owe their lives this day to the extraordinary hurry in which Lane's Brigade was that morning to "bust a cap!"

After this, a pretty short skirmish commenced and continued for an hour or two, when the enemy finding it impossible to effect a crossing, ceased firing and maneuvered so skillfully as to disguise their retreat. Gen. Stuart suspecting their intentions had hastily withdrawn Lomax's Brigade and marched rapidly up the river about five miles to Liberty Mills, where he was joined by a Brigade of Infantry under Genl. [Brigadier General Samuel] McGowan. Crossing over on an excellent covered bridge, which spans the river at that point, we moved briskly on towards the road by which the enemy had advanced that morning, hoping to fall upon the flank of their retreating columns; but they had been too fast for us, and we had the poor satisfaction only of driving off their rear-guard from behind their freshly constructed barricades. Getting into the road leading back to Barnett's ford we bade Genl. McGowan good evening and crossed the river about dusk on our return to camp, arriving there in time for a good supper, which it is needless to say was heartily enjoyed after the fatigues of the day.

About the 1st of March, 1864, Lomax's Brigade which had been doing all the picket duty at the fords on the upper Rapidan, and even as far out as Madison Court House was relieved by the 1st and 2nd Virginia Cavalry, the portion of Wickham's Brigade which was the first to report to duty after being disbanded at Xmas. Gen. Wickham himself was in command and established his Headquarters not far from Montpelier, the old residence of James Madison. It was not long before our repose was broken by an ugly report from the picket line that the Yankee Cavalry were again on the war-path, and this time still further to our left, crossing the headwaters of the Rapidan in the vicinity of Wolftown. Again ensued another scene of mounting in hot haste, and in a few moments we were galloping thro' Orange Court House en route for Wickham's Headquarters. Arriving there Gen. Stuart ordered that officer to follow him with his whole available force. One of his regts. was on picket so we had to start with only the 2nd Virginia Cavalry and Co. K. of the 1st Virginia — a Maryland Co. commanded by Capt. [Captain George R.] Gaither.

The day which had been unusually bright and balmy, towards its close gave promise of bad weather, and sure enough, before nightfall a heavy snow-storm set in. Passing thro' Barboursville we turned off towards Charlottesville in which direction we had fancied we heard during the evening the sound of artillery firing. After marching until near 10 o'clock P.M. and arriving as we thought within 10 miles of Charlottesville the column was halted and a report received that Major [sic] Breathed and McGregor had repulsed an attack of [Brigadier General George A.] Custer's Brigade that evening on their camp of Artillery and that the enemy were then retreating slowly in the direction of Stanardsville. Gen. Stuart called Major Venable aside, and after a short whispered conversation, Venable rode by us in the dark, remarking to me as he passed: "Good-bye, my boy, — I'm off for Charlottesville. Would you like to go?" "Yes," I said, "above all things." But there was no such good luck for me. Counter-marching the column a short distance, Gen. Stuart having procured a good guide, struck out across the country by a route which certainly had never been traveled before, and I trust, may never have to be traveled by me again. We seemed, if anything, to avoid all roads as much as possible, and having neither Artillery or Ambulances to bring along, we went as rapidly as the horses could possibly go. The night was intensely dark, and the snow having changed to a heavy sleet, made the march much harder on man & beast. Not a soul, save Gen. Stuart and his guide, knew where we were going, but there was a very strong suspicion in our minds that we were looking for Yankees. The tramp was kept up for three or four hours, when suddenly the column was halted, and an order passed down the line to "form fours." What! — a charge? — in all this mud and darkness? No. The men were next ordered to dismount, and about two hundred cold and shivering troopers trudged by me with their carbines unslung, going to the front. They were halted and deployed along the line of a rail fence, with orders not to speak a word or make the slightest noise. In utter ignorance of our whereabouts, I asked one after another of our staff but could get no information. Presently, Ben Weller came up and informed me that we were then alongside of the main road from Stanardsville to Wolftown on which Custer's whole Brigade was retreating; that we had cut 'em off and were now going to ambush them as they passed along before us. No sound, save the rattle of the sleet on the trees around us, could be heard as we strained our ears & eyes thro' the darkness for the first sound or sign of the approaching enemy. An hour passed away. Suddenly the loud report of a single carbine rang out thro' the woods breaking the awful stillness, and startling every man to brace himself more firmly in the saddle, and grasp his pistol with a tighter grip. A solitary prisoner was then brought in, who could give no account of himself, being as ignorant as we were of the position of his command. Not another shot was fired, and getting tired of waiting, we dismounted and built a fire in the road. Gen. Stuart and Gen. Wickham both stretched themselves out on rails near the fire, while their respective staffs made themselves as comfortable as was possible under the circumstances and it was not long before every one of us was fast asleep.

A scouting party, a Lieut. and 8 men of the 2nd Virginia Cavalry had been sent up the road towards Stanardsville, and just about daybreak one of these men came back and reported that his Lieut. had ridden up to a squad of Yankees at Stanardsville but had been forced to retire on them showing fight. As soon as this was told Gen. Stuart, he ordered Wickham to mount his command and move towards Stanardsville. The bugler of the 2nd at once started to blow "Boots & Saddles" but was choked before he had gotten far into that martial air, by the utterance of many "damns," and other signs of disapproval from his comrades, who knew that this was no place for such music. Off we started, and getting into the rockiest road in the world, moved on at a brisk trot. Co. K. 1st Virginia Cavalry was in front, and after travelling less than a mile from our "ambush," met a squadron of Custer's Brigade coming toward them. Gen. Stuart at once ordered a "Charge," and in another moment the Yankees were retreating at full speed, and orders were sent to the 2nd Regiment then commanded by Major Cary Breckenridge [sic] to come up at a gallop.

In less than five minutes, Co. K. was seen hurrying back closely followed by a charging squadron of Yankees, which was only induced to draw rein at sight of our advancing column. But now the range of hills in our front was literally swarming with Yankee cavalry, which deployed right and left on either side of the road, and pushed forward a heavy line of skirmishers. A corn-crib stood in the field on the left of the road near which a few of our mounted men were making a stand. Gen. Stuart sent me to them with orders to hold on there till the very last minute and encourage them with the hope of speedy re-inforcement. I rode in among them, shouting to them to stand firm, and at the same time firing my revolver into a column of Yankees which had pushed up to the corn-crib and were letting us have it at short range, not 150 yards distant in a plain open field. While busy firing into this body of the enemy, I heard Gen. Wickham's voice close behind me, and turning, saw him ride up on his powerful bay horse, and order the men to rally, as they were getting scattered, and some had already stuck spurs and fled. The Yankees were now getting ready to dash upon us, and in another moment they commenced a charge. After a parting salute, our little squad, having made the best stand they could, wheeled and ran. There was but one opening in the rail fence which surrounded the field, by which we could escape, and I shall never forget the uncomfortable sound of those Yankee carbine balls as they whistled over our backs when we crowded through the gap. To my amazement they failed to hit a man or a horse, and I turned around after getting through the fence to observe a dozen Yankees within 20 paces, yelling "Surrender" at the top of their voices. This same party galloped their horses along the fence until they came within easy pistol shot of Gen. Stuart and Capt. Grattan, to whom they gave chase. The General seeing that they could not get at him over the fence, cantered along down the lane rather too leisurely, turning every now and then to his ordnance officer and saying, "Shoot that fellow, Grattan! Shoot him!" pointing to a Yankee who was plugging away at them both. But instead of Grattan shooting him, the Yankee shot Grattan's horse, inflicting a severe wound in his hind-quarters and laming him for the rest of the day. As I galloped away from my pursuers I came near having a serious mishap. My horse, jaded and worn out, plunged both fore-feet into a rotten stump-hole; his nose was bumped hard against the ground, and I was thrown far up on his neck, but gathering himself up he had the strength to rise, and scrambling back into the saddle, I continued my retreat.

Seeing our little command scatter in every direction, (we had only about 300 men; Custer had at least 1500 and a battery of artillery) I endeavored to rejoin Gen. Stuart, but getting into an unknown road I lost all reckoning, and being ignorant of the country, rode on till I found a house and made such inquiries as enabled me to know what to do. As I travelled along thro' the rain, with my oilcloth over my shoulder, and an india-rubber cover over my cap, I noticed a horseman behind me approaching leisurely tho' gaining on me, as I walked my horse over the rough and slippery road. When he had gotten within ten feet of me, he cried out in a rather excited tone "Halt there"! Turning, I was surprised to see his carbine cocked and pointing at my head. At the same time the stranger remarked "Halt sir, you're my prisoner"! Said I "What command do you belong to"? "Second Virginia" was the reply. "Oh! well" said I, "I reckon you're mistaken about my being your prisoner". "No, I aint [sic] either", said he, "and if you don't give me your arms pretty quick, I'll blow your brains out for you". "Look here, my friend", I answered, "You must quit this foolishness, I'm no Yankee" and throwing aside my oilcloth I showed him my Confederate uniform. But he was not convinced even by this, so we rode along together in no very amicable mood. Meeting Capt. Henry Lee, one of Gen. Fitz Lee's staff officers, who was then on a visit to Army Hdqrs, and now in charge of a party of the "S. G. & C", my would-be captor left me, very sorry no doubt that he hadn't made a bona-fide Yankee prisoner of me.

Capt. Lee informed me that Gen. R.E. Lee, with nearly all of A.P. Hill's Corps, was on the road leading from Jack's Shop to Madison Court House and added that he thought it would be well for me to report to him what had happened. I determined at once to do so, and after a ride of four or five miles struck the road on which our infantry was marching and soon found Gen. Lee.

Some confusion took place as I rode up, the cause of which I do not now recollect, but my impression is that a line of battle had been formed in an awkward position near the River, and Gen. Lee had ordered it to be changed, and while the movement was being executed, a rumor was circulated that a column of the enemy was crossing over to attack. I was utterly at a loss to understand the situation, not having heard that any Yankee Infantry had moved out, and I am ignorant to this day what was the cause of our bringing out such a heavy force. In a short time, Genl. Stuart himself rode up, and he & Genl. Lee went into close conversation. Nothing further was heard from the enemy till near dark, when scouts came in reporting that Custer had crossed back to his side of the river at Wolftown and their infantry column had disappeared from our front. I presume that Gen. Meade (or Gen. Grant, for I am uncertain whether Meade was still in command) hearing of the attempt to intercept Custer, had made a demonstration against our left with a heavy body of infantry, thus necessitating a corresponding movement by Genl. Lee.

Snow fell during the night, but as we had our quarters in an old cabin it didn't interfere with our slumbers, which were heavier than usual on account of the almost entire lack of sleep on the previous night. The sun rose beautifully bright and clear next morning, and at an early hour we commenced our homeward march. Passing the Infantry on the road, we cantered briskly along the frozen road, undisturbed by anything save the thought of breakfast which had to be deferred until we reached camp. It was near 1 o'clock before we alighted in front of our tents, and with appetites whetted by long fasting, we took two meals in one by having an early dinner. Gen. Stuart, as I have said elsewhere, was an ardent lover of coffee, drinking it three times a day, and I well remember the zest with which, on this occasion, he emptied and replenished the silver cup from which he invariably drank the delicious beverage.

All hands were too tired to do much more than swallow their rations, and I thought I observed on Stuart's countenance a more serious expression then I had ever seen there. It was evident that he didn't think well of the past two days' proceedings, and that he was chafing under the restraint which the absence of his command placed upon him. If Wickham's whole brigade, instead of one fourth of it, had only been with him, Custer would have had a rough time on that rocky road.

We had scarcely finished dinner when a dispatch was handed to Gen. Stuart after reading which, he ordered a fresh horse to be saddled, and in less time than it takes me to write it he was off again with only two or three of the Staff. This time it was a report that Kilpatrick had broken thro' our lines on the extreme right, and was then on a raid towards Richmond. Several of the Staff, having shifted their saddles from their tired horses' backs to other and fresher animals rode off with the General, but I was so unfortunate as to not have a re-mount, and he therefore bade me to remain in camp, give my horse a good rest and follow him the next day. Major Venable arrived in camp that evening on his return from Charlottesville, and the next morning after an early breakfast we started off together to join Gen. Stuart. Getting into the Fredericksburg Plank Road we journeyed briskly on in the direction of Verdiersville, at which place we had heard that Gen. Stuart had spent the night. This, it will be remembered by all who have read von Borcke's narrative, was the place where the enemy once caught the General napping, carrying off as a trophy his grey felt hat and black flowing plume, together with a little ornament which he prized more highly perhaps than anything else about it; this was a palmetto rosette, plaitted [sic] by a fair daughter of the South, and caught up with a small braid of her own hair, which Gen. Stuart had constantly worn on that hat. The lady herself was not personally known to him, but he wore it for the sake of one who had honored him as her own champion and protector.[30] Passing Verdiersville, we learned that Gen. Stuart had left there early that morning, going towards Chancellorsville; we therefore pressed on after him. Getting beyond Parker's Store we came up with a Battery of Artillery, toiling along the muddy road (the 2nd Company of Richmond Howitzers) and I learned from some of my friends in the Company that a

Brigade or two of [Lieutenant General Richard S.] Ewell's Corps was on the road a few miles ahead of us. Before reaching Chancellorsville we came upon Gen. Stuart, with Maj. McClellan, Capt. Grattan and Lieut. R.E. Lee, Jr., together with half a dozen of the escort under Lieut. Hagan.[31] McClellan was writing dispatches at the Genl's dictation as we rode up. I saluted, dismounted and was tying my horse to the limb of a tree, when I received an order from Genl. Stuart to ride on down to the old Chancellorsville Tavern and deliver a message (an unimportant one) to the officer in command of the Infantry there. I believe it was simply directing that officer to go into camp and to return next day to their old camp in Orange County, as there was then no enemy within thirty miles of them. It had been ascertained that Kilpatrick and Col. [Colonel Ulric] Dahlgren were knocking about in the vicinity of Richmond, and our fears were excited lest they might perpetrate a successful raid into the heart of that city. Gen. Hampton with a very small force of cavalry was encamped for the winter near Bowling Green, in Caroline County, and could only offer a feeble resistance to the heavy force which Kilpatrick had with him, then variously estimated at from 5000 to 10,000 mounted men. Before leaving our Hdqrs. a telegram had been sent to Gen. Rosser who was expected to reach Gordonsville that day with his Brigade being then on the march from Lexington to join his Division. A courier was also dispatched to meet him at Orange Springs with orders to hurry on eastward as rapidly as possible. We all thought, of course, that we were going to bivouac alongside of the plank-road and wait for Rosser's Brigade to join us. But no, the General had a far different intention. Just as we had commenced making preparations for the night, looking up forage for our weary horses etc., we heard General Stuart sing out in a lively tone, "Well Gentlemen, Come ahead — who's going with me?" and in another moment he had swung himself into the saddle and was moving off. We followed him wondering what route he would take, and soon found ourselves moving due south. It was rapidly growing dark and getting colder every second, the biting March wind whistling thro' the bare limbs or rustling the crisp leaves on the ground as we passed thro' the Wilderness. After riding about an hour we halted at a house; I have forgotten the owner's name but Gen. Stuart seeming to be well acquainted with the whole family, dismounted and went inside. They were (not far from the Old Furnace) people whose acquaintances he had formed when he had piloted Gen. Jackson around on that memorable march against the left {Side notation: ?} flank of Hooker's Army at Chancellorsville.[32] All of our staff entered the house, and we sat for a short while around a cheerful fire warming ourselves & discussing the probabilities of remaining in these comfortable quarters for the night. Our host set out a decanter of apple-brandy of which some of the elder members of the staff partook, while I with youthful modesty, paid such deference to my General's known aversion to ardent spirits as to forgo the pleasure of drinking with them. I shall never forget the loss of that drink, for tho' I very rarely indulged, yet I am sure it would have helped to "keep the cold out" during the long and severe ride which lay before us. We spent only about fifteen minutes at the house and remounting, followed our leader who had by this time informed us that we must reach Hanover Junction before sunrise. Now Hanover Junction was nearly forty miles distant. But we pushed on, and did accomplished the distance by 7 o'clock next morning, stopping only once on the way, at Dr. Flippo's on the Telegraph Road. This then made upwards of 75 miles for Maj. Venable's horse and mine, travelled within less than 24 hours and without once stopping to be fed!

The night was intensely cold, but notwithstanding it, the constant riding of the three previous days made every one of us heavy with sleep; I well remember how Gen. Stuart would fall to napping on his horse, while Lieut. Lee and myself, on either side of him, held him by the sleeve of his jacket to keep him steady in the saddle, as mile after mile of the weary way was overcome. At Dr. Flippo's we dismounted & entered the house, rousing the Doctor from his warm bed about 3 AM; he at once kindled a blazing fire in the dining room, and yielding to its somniferous influence, our whole party dropped asleep on chairs, on the floor, anywhere! Gen. Stuart made a pillow out of my body as I leaned on the dining table, and he too went fast asleep. Lieut. Lee with his back against the wall and his knees drawn up to his forehead slept peacefully and profoundly, while every now and then a yawn or a groan from some one would but faintly indicate the pursuit of slumber "under difficulty." But in less than a half hour, Stuart shook us all up and we were again in the saddle en route for the Junction.

We soon came up with two or three stragglers from Rosser's Brigade which had passed into the road a few miles ahead of us. These men were warming themselves at a fire they had just built on the roadside, and it did seem hard to make the poor fellows mount their horses and push on to rejoin their command, tho' they were fortunate perhaps in escaping with this slight punishment.

It will be remembered by those of our party that night who survived the war, that very soon after this we encountered along the road that most offensive of all odors which can assail human olfactories, emitted by that abominable little creature, known to naturalists as the <u>Mephitis Americana</u>. This perfume actually <u>pervaded</u> the atmosphere for two or three miles of the way; and when we arrived at Han. Junction the cause was there ascertained. One of these animals had paid its respects to Gen. Rosser's Aid-de-camp who was riding at the head of the column, and the unfortunate staff officer had been furnished with a <u>week's</u> leave of absence to recover from the effects of his <u>wound</u>. We hope to be pardoned for the insertion of this reminiscence here, but it came near causing serious sickness to some of our party, and is therefore made memorable, and deemed admissible as a part of the <u>res gestae</u>.

But it is time we were hearing something of the enemy. A report reached us at Hanover Junction that Gen. Hampton, with his usual vigilance and dash, had made a successful night attack upon a camp of Yankee Cavalry near Atlee's Station on the Virginia Central Railroad, routing them, and continuing the pursuit toward the lower Chickahominy. It was also rumored that the famous Col. Dahlgren had been killed by one of our scouting parties under Lieut. P. [Lieutenant James Pollard] of the 9th Virginia Cavalry.[33] Here then, our march was ended. Being in the neighborhood of Cedar Hill (my home) I invited Gen. Stuart and the staff and as many of the couriers as would accompany us to make it their Headquarters. They accepted and we continued our ride one mile beyond the Depot, arriving at the house in time for breakfast. The horses were put away in the stable, and it was determined to rest during the day. The next morning we took the train at 9 o'clock for Gordonsville, leaving our horses in charge of Lieut. Hagan and the couriers, to be brought to camp overland. We reached our camp at Orange Court House that evening, and Hagan arrived with the horses the next day.

Shortly after this we were all invited to a Grand Tournament and Ball, given by the officers of the 3rd Corps — A.P. Hill's. The Tournament took place in an open field alongside the Orange & Alexandria Railroad not far from the residence of Maj. John H. Lee. The Knights, who by the way, were all officers of the Infantry (Cavalryman having been ruled out) had been practising themselves and horses for weeks before the trial of skill took place, and had reached a degree of proficiency truly admirable. The task they had set themselves was no easy one. I forget the exact length of the lists, not more than a 150 yards in all which distance had to be made in a very few seconds — so short a time indeed as to keep the horse at full speed; and at this gait the rider was to cut off with a "right cut" a head pretty firmly fastened on a post about five feet in height, then with his sabre at "tierce point" take the ring which was suspend'd about twenty yards before him, next and at the same interval of distance with a right cut against Infantry "take off" a head elevated only a foot from the ground, and finally with his sabre at "carte point" pierce and carry off a head situated similarly as the first. About thirty Knights, all handsomely dressed and equipped, and beautifully mounted, made their entrance, amid the applause of a multitude of spectators and the inspiring strains of martial music, received their charge, and commenced the struggle for that most alluring of all earthly prizes — a woman's smile. I cannot recollect now who was declared the winner, nor who received from their brave Knight the honor of being crowned Queen of Love and Beauty. I remember tho' that the fair sex were especially pleased with the day's performance, and the whole assembly dispersed well satisfied with the display. Several of us remained behind and amused ourselves trying the mettle of our horses at a high fence near at hand, and more than one of us received some memorable falls.

Within a few days after the Tournament, the Ball was announced to take place at the Marye House, what had once been the seat of wealth and refinement, then occupied by its owner, situated a few miles north of the Court House I shall not undertake to describe this Ball; those who were present will remember it all their lives; and those who were not would have some difficulty in appreciating the situation. Gen. Stuart was too busy to attend, so he sent Venable, Fontaine and myself into the darkness and leaving "the banquet hall deserted." As I was riding along with Dr. Fontaine and Maj. Venable I heard a voice, as of some one in great pain, calling out thro' the darkness: "Atwell! Oh! Atwell!" Riding down alongside a deep gulley [sic] which ran near the road & parallel to it we called out towards the place whence the voice came, for it was too dark to see anything, and soon ascertained that the wounded man was no other than our friend General H.____ whose horse, a wild and ungovernable animal, had pranced into this deep ditch and fallen with him, happily however inflicting only a few severe bruises. Helping the General out we soon put him in the hands of some of his staff who had not yet ridden off, and bidding them all goodnight, made the best of our way to our quarters.[34] We received next morning a reprimand from Genl. Stuart for being late at breakfast, the severity of which however was tempered by the telling him of the many regrets we had heard expressed at his absence, some ladies having declared that they "would not have attended the ball if they had not thought they would see General Stuart."

Time wore on without any event worth recording. The different members of the staff were each in turn the recipients of "boxes from home" containing old hams, turkies [sic], vegetables, sweetmeats and other good things of this life, which contributed most materially to the general larder of the mess. A resolution was passed, probably out of consideration for the "Junior Member," as they used to call me, restricting our mess-bill to $100 each per month. As my pay was only $130, $10 of which went to my servant, I had not a very extensive margin for sundries to go upon. One day about the time of the receipt of one of the largest of these "boxes," we invited Gen. R.E. Lee and staff to dine with us. He accepted and we prepared a royal dinner for him, but we were only disappointed by receiving only his "regrets" a few minutes before dinner was announced, tho' he sent three of his staff officers over to represent him. We enjoyed their society, and they enjoyed our dinner, if a good appetite is any sign on such occasions.

A pleasant variation of the monotony of camplife was the visit, about this time, of Gov. Z. [Zebulon] B. Vance of North Carolina, on a tour of speech-making to the North Carolina Brigades scattered thro' the different Divisions of the Army. I had the pleasure of hearing him once at the "meeting-house" of [Major General Robert E.] Rodes' Division, and again when he addressed the men of Lane's Brigade. As a stump-speaker and narrator of good "yarns,"

Gov. Vance can hardly be excelled and he was rec'd on this occasion with shouts of enthusiasm and applause by the North Carolina soldiers wherever he went.

(July 14, 1872 — I had the pleasure of hearing Gov. Vance address a Political Meeting at Weldon today. He made a powerful appeal to the North Carolinians to vote down the oppression & corruption of the Radical thieves who are now ruining the State. About 1500 people were present and great enthusiasm manifested for the Greeley and Brown Ticket! Think of that; Compare Vance in 1864 and Vance in 1872. *"Tempora ruitantur, et nos mutamur in illis."*)

But it is time now to turn to other themes. Two months of Spring had already passed by, and the expectation of an early movement was hourly increasing. Every visit to our fair friends was paid in sad anticipation that the hour of final farewell was drawing nigh, and each "good-bye" was whispered as tho' it were our last. Sunday was the 1st of May, and on the 2nd, our little party had planned, with the assistance of some of our brethren of the Infantry, Staff officers A.P. Hill's Corps, a May-Party for the young ladies of Orange. Pegram had borrowed the Headquarters Ambulance, which the Genl. kindly put at his disposal, bidding us express to the ladies his regrets at not being able to accompany us. I mounted my horse and with two or three of my friends galloped over to Major Lee's, where we were to take on our fair freight, and thence set out for Montpelier, the place chosen for the pic-nic, or May-party. This place was then in the occupancy of a family from Maryland, whose name I have forgotten. We drove up with two or three ambulance loads of young ladies, and were received most hospitably and kindly. Our brass band, the band of [Brigadier General Ambrose R.] Wright's Georgia Brigade, soon commenced discoursing sweet music, and selecting our partners for the dance, we entered the spacious hall of Montpelier, and for hours tripped the "light fantastic," unmindful of aught save the happiness of the moment, irreverently treading the same floors which during the First Rebellion had been paced by the feet of the "Father of the Constitution."

We had brought with us ample provision for the inner man, and woman too, and after a hearty lunch which all seemed to enjoy, we adjourned to the parlor, and were treated to some delightful music, both vocal and instrumental, by two or three of the ladies of our party. As evening drew on, the party began to separate and by sunset we had returned the ladies to their respective homes, and were on our way to camp.

I remarked to Pegram as we rode along together: "I feel that this is the last time we'll meet those ladies; I'll bet you we will move tomorrow." Not so, however, for we remained quiet on Tuesday, tho' there was a rumor that the enemy were about to cross the River, and sure enough, on Tuesday night the 3rd of May we rec'd marching orders.

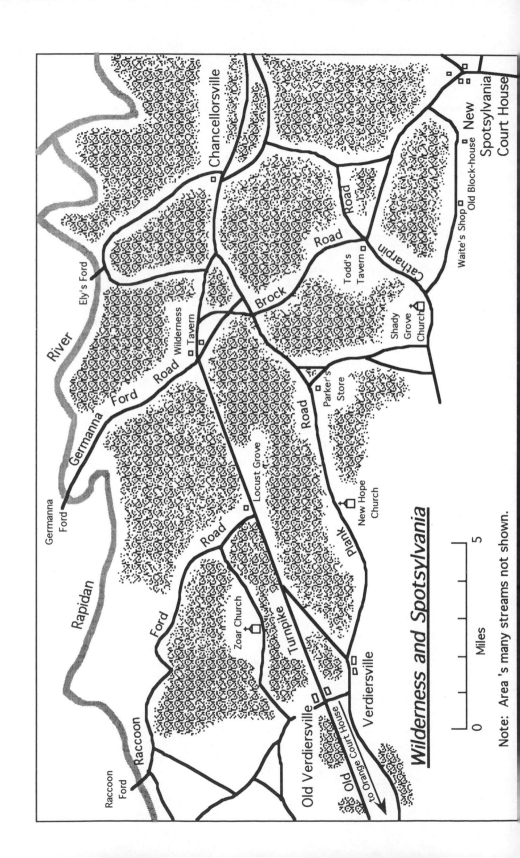

Wilderness and Spotsylvania

Note: Area 's many streams not shown.

0   Miles   5

Rapidan

Germanna Ford

Raccoon Ford

River

Ely's Ford

Germanna Ford Road

Raccoon Ford Road

Chancellorsville

Wilderness Tavern

Brock Road

Locust Grove

Plank Road

New Hope Church

Parker's Store

Todd's Tavern

Catharpin Road

Shady Grove Church

Zoar Church

Turnpike

Old Verdiersville

Verdiersville

Old Court House

to Orange Court House

Waite's Shop

Old Block-house

New Spotsylvania Court House

I make no apology for letting my memory dwell with sad retrospect upon this breaking up of "Camp Wigwam" — the last regular camp that Gen. Stuart ever made. I had begun to have a real home-feeling for the old place. The happy hours we had all spent there, had endeared everything about it to me, and I confess that I witnessed the striking of our tents and the packing of our baggage with a certain feeling of regret, which however was soon overcome amid the hurry and bustle of our departure. And yet, even at this distant day, I turn with a sad longing, and contemplate the scene, fraught with such ominous significance, the rude severance of tender ties and pleasing recollections, and I wonder if I can ever again be as lighthearted and happy as when on that old campground.[35]

Gen. Stuart sent me with a message to Army Headquarters, and I had the honor of being admitted for the first time into the tent of our beloved Commander in Chief — Gen. R. E. Lee. He was alone, and received me with that calm, easy, indescribable grace which put to flight the feeling of fear and trembling without which it was almost impossible for a youth like myself to come into his presence. No sign of haste or impatience was visible on his countenance, or in his majestic manner and noble bearing, and no one could have imagined that he was going to pass anything more than a peaceful, quiet morning, in the solitude of his tent; I had just given him the information, which however I dare say had reached him before, that the enemy were in motion for the lower fords of the Rapidan. The whole of our Army was getting under arms and in marching order, and Genl. Lee's Headquarters were about to be changed from this quiet grove of pines, to the uncertain bivouac in the Wilderness of Spotsylvania.

In a few moments, I heard the tramp of Cavalry, and Genl. Stuart rode up. He dismounted and after a brief interview with Gen. Lee, remounted and set out on the Plank Road towards Verdiersville. Continuing our march down to Parker's Store we went into camp there. The next morning, May 5th, we were up bright and early, and found ourselves in the midst of heavy columns of Infantry who were marching down toward the Brock Road. Gen. Stuart had no Cavalry immediately with him. Rosser's Brigade with some of the Horse Artillery was off on our right, on the Catharpin Road. Chambliss's Brigade had been left in Orange County with orders to cross over into Culpeper as soon as the enemy left their camps there, and destroy any stores they might leave behind them. Gen. Fitz Lee with his Division, Lomax's & Wickham's Brigades, had been stationed in the neighborhood of Hamilton's Crossing, while Genl Hampton with the remnant of Young's & Gordon's Brigade was at or near Guiney's Station. Gen. Stuart ordered these several commands to move up as rapidly as possible and take position on the right of the Army.

And now commenced the series of movements known in history as "the Battles in the Wilderness."

I cannot pretend to a sufficientcy [sic] of knowledge or accuracy of recollection to give any detailed account of these fights. I can only state the general impression they made on my mind; the monotony of that story may perchance be relieved by the description of certain events of which I can claim to have been an eye witness.

[Major General Henry] Heth's Division, I think, was in front that morning and Genl. Stuart advanced with a small body of skirmishers to the vicinity of the Brock Road. Near this point we came up with the enemy's advance-guard and light skirmishing began. The Wilderness here is so dense and impenetrable that nothing can be seen. The consequence was that the skirmish lines were brought in close proximity to each other, and whenever a shot was fired at such short range, somebody was apt to get hurt. As soon as the firing commenced, the main body of the Infantry on both sides, moved up and formed lines of battle. Just where our first line was formed, across the plank road, and on the left hand side of that road there was an open field, part of which had once been an orchard. It sloped gradually away about 200 yards down to the edge of a thick piece of woods — a sort of broom-straw oasis in this Wilderness of black-jacks, willow-oaks and stunted pines.

Genl. Lee & staff, Gens. [Brigadier General William N.] Pendleton, Stuart, and perhaps other General & field officers were all collected in this field and were chatting leisurely, some dismounted, holding their bridles in hand and letting their horses crop the tender shoots and blades of grass which the early Spring was then bringing into life; others discussing the position, and the reported movement of the enemy in our front, and all as unmindful & careless of danger as tho' about to go on drill or witness a General Review; when all at once, a skirmish line of Blue-coats emerged slowly & cautiously from the wood at the foot of the field, in full view and close range of the whole party. For a moment, we gazed at them, and they at us, in mute astonishment. Then all eyes & minds were turned toward General Lee, who was sitting on his horse, looking over a map, still talking with the group of officers about him, unconscious of the enemy's presence. A little stir in the crowd was created, as those of us who were dismounted endeavored to regain our saddles, expecting every second to be greeted with a certain & destructive volley. But no; the same astonishment which had befallen us, seemed to fill their minds, and to our infinite amazement, we beheld them, " 'bout face," and sink back under the thick cover without firing a single shot, disappearing from view as quietly, and as mysteriously I might say, as they had come. A body of our skirmishers was at once deployed and moved down toward the wood where the enemy's line had appeared. They were soon lost to view in the forest, tho' a dropping fire was shortly afterward heard which announced their encounter with the other party.[36]

Soon after this, a courier rode up with a message for Genl. Stuart from Genl. Rosser, announcing the beginning of a skirmish between his Brigade of Cavalry and [Brigadier General James H.] Wilson's Division of Federal Cavalry which was trying to force its way up the Catharpin Road, on our extreme right. Gen. Stuart, bidding his Staff & Escort to remain where they were, and taking with him only one or two officers and two couriers, rode rapidly over to the Catharpin Road to join Gen. Rosser and witness the fight. He arrived just as Rosser's Brigade had repulsed a dashing charge of Wilson's men, and was preparing himself to follow up the success. Moving up all his mounted men rapidly, and ordering the Horse Arty forward at a gallop, Rosser made a dash at the enemy in his front, and succeeded in breaking their line. They fell back in confusion and disorder, giving up their advanced position on the flank of the Army and retiring 3 or 4 miles, to the vicinity of Todd's Tavern.

Gen. Stuart then returned to the Plank Road to consult with Genl. Lee. When we arrived there we found Heth's Division hotly engaged. They had been fighting for two or three hours and it was now nearly sunset. Some misunderstanding of orders had occurred, and just as we rode up, the scene immediately in rear of our lines was anything but encouraging. It seemed that one of Heth's Brigades had been sent in to relieve one that had been under fire all the evening. The Brigade that was on the line mistook the order, and commenced retiring before the other one had time to occupy their places, and in passing each other in the dense undergrowth, they became considerably mixed up and thrown out of order. Just then the enemy raised a yell and rushed forward. For a few minutes the firing was terrific. The brigade that was retiring came swarming out in alarm, while the fresh brigade was pressed almost beyond endurance. General Lee, who was only a short distance behind the line, and fully exposed to this heavy fire, rode in among the retreating crowd and in his calm, steady, dignified tone, told one after another "Go back, boys" — "Go back!" "we want you in front now." Cols. Venable, Taylor and others of the Staff, remonstrated with Gen. Lee for this unnecessary exposure of himself. But the grand old man wouldn't leave until he saw his men returning to their work.[37]

Gen. Stuart and his staff set to work also gathering up fugitives, who by the way, seemed perfectly willing to return, having as several of them told me at the time, thought that they had been ordered to "come out." It was a warm close evening, and I shall never forget the appearance of those men, with their hands and faces begrimed with powder, panting for breath and calling out all around me for water, of which unfortunately there was none to be had near the battle ground.

The line was restored about dark and the troops bivouacked in line of battle. Gen. Stuart and staff spent the night near Parker's Store.[38]

The next morning, May 6th, Gen. Stuart joined General Rosser, and about 10 A.M. ordered that officer to take his brigade down into the Wilderness by a road leading off from the Catharpin Road and between that and the Plank

Road, aiming to strike the left flank of the enemy's Infantry and ascertain their position and probable movements. The brigade had been in motion about a half-hour when Genl. Stuart, who was in rear of the column & unable to pass it owing to the narrowness of the road, gave me an order to deliver to Gen. Rosser to the following effect — the enemy's outposts would shortly be reached, and Gen. Rosser was directed to "go at them, on sight." The woods were very thick, and I forced my horse with difficulty past the long files of Rosser's Brigade, and fortunately reached the head of the column in good time. Delivering my message, I halted to await Gen' Stuart's arrival. The order had been sent on to the advance guard, and in a few minutes I heard sharp firing, and then a yell resounded thro' the forest which assured that it was being obeyed to the very letter. The whole column then struck a trot, and as we descended a hill, at the foot of which was a considerable stream, we met some wounded men coming back, among whom I recognized my friend Capt. Hugh McGuire, slightly wounded in the arm. Pushing on with Gen. Stuart who had arrived, we entered some open fields, where the ground was very rolling, and found quite a skirmish going on with a small force of Federal Cavalry. McGregor's Battery was hurried forward to a good position on one of the hills and commenced a duel with a Yankee Battery off to our right. One of the enemy's guns was dismounted at the first fire, and the rest of his battery driven back a short distance. Whereupon, McGregor limbered up his guns, drove forward at a gallop and occupied another hill still nearer to the enemy. A considerable force of dismounted men was posted to protect our battery, and a desultory fire was kept up for about an hour. Gen. Stuart busied himself observing the enemy's lines, and Gen. Rosser threw forward a body of skirmishers into a thick piece of undergrowth on our left. Towards our left and rear, and about a half a mile distant we could see the enemy's Infantry clustered about near a farm house, and soon we saw them drive up a battery and go into position. All was quiet however for a few minutes longer — but suddenly they advanced upon us in front, and at the same moment the batteries on both of our flanks opened on us, their own shell crossing each other in mid-air, and spreading considerable alarm in our ranks. There was nothing left for us but to retreat, and we came out hastily, tho' without much confusion and with scarcely any loss.

Gen. Stuart retreated only a short distance, halting after it was discovered that the enemy showed no disposition to press us back. After waiting on the road an hour or two, he determined to attack them again in the same place, and Gen. Rosser was led back to the same ground. A similar repulse was met with, and this time it came near being a serious affair. As we were coming out of this "man-trap," Gen. Stuart told me to ride across to the Plank Road and tell Gen. Lee what had been taking place, describing our position and the enemy's, and to bring back information as to how the fight along the lines had gone, heavy firing having been heard in that direction all the morning. Leaving Gen. Stuart on his way out, I plunged into the Wilderness, with nothing to guide me, save a very vague, general knowledge of the position of the two armies. I could discover no sign of a road nor even a hog-path, as I urged my jaded horse thro' the thick undergrowth of knotty black-jacks and small thorny oaks. A heavy cloud of smoke had settled down over the Wilderness, caused by the fires which were raging all over the battlefield rendering it impossible to see anything at a distance of twenty yards. As I made my way thro' these woods I could hear a loud, roaring noise, resembling somewhat the sound of a wagon-train on a rough road, and growing louder and louder as I advanced. I fancied it was caused by the enemy's heavy trains on the Old Plank Road, and imagined that I was approaching too near their lines. But the reader may judge of my surprise and alarm when I suddenly saw coming thro' the woods a line of fire about four feet in height and stretching, as I supposed, indefinitely in either direction, driven swiftly before a high wind, licking up the dried grass and dead leaves with seeming insatiable fury & scorching everything in its path into black and shapeless masses. Right onwards the flames rushed towards me, leaping and hissing like a thousand serpents with tongues of fire and causing the timber to crackle & crash in its fall with a sound like the rattle of musketry. My horse stopped short and snorted with fear, and the next moment wheeled suddenly around in his tracks to escape what seemed to be a very serious danger. And so it was, owing to the fact that it was impossible to ride out of a walk in the jungle. I spurred him back however a short distance and then commenced trying to flank the fire. After riding a few hundred yards along its front, I came to a place where it had burned low and leaping my horse over a little light blaze, I gained its rear and endeavored to put myself in the right course to reach the Plank Road. The sun was sufficiently hot, without the aid of this immense fire, to make my ride extremely uncomfortable; add to this the scratching of both hands and face by the sharp, thorny branches of the scorched trees and you can form some idea of my troubles. Riding on I came to a steep rocky mound, some twenty feet high and determined to scale it, if possible, and from its top take a view of the surrounding country. In my effort to ride up its steep sides, my sabre was jerked entirely out of its scabbard and left hanging on a bush behind me. I had to dismount and recover it. My clothing was badly torn, and altogether I was in woeful condition. Reaching the top of this little hill, I cast my eyes around the horizon, but could see nothing but smoke in every direction. The firing had ceased along the lines, so I had nothing whatever to guide me in choosing a route out of this wild region. As I made my way down from the hill a wild turkey ran off before me, and I involuntarily drew my pistol to take a shot at her, but she disappeared in the thicket. Following the direction of the turkey, I was brought into an old worn-out cart-track into which I turned with a feeling of considerable relief, determined not to risk another encounter with either the fire or the forest. A ride of about twenty minutes brought me to one of our vidette posts, and from them I obtained directions how to reach the Plank Road. I soon found Gen. Lee and reported. The General took great interest in my message, and made me walk off with him to the foot of an apple-tree in the old broom-straw field (described above) and there sitting down he opened a map on which he made me trace the roads and show him exactly where Gen. Stuart was when I left him. This I did as well as I was able, and then rec'g a message from Gen. Lee for Gen. Stuart, I started on my return. Found Gen. Stuart at a farmhouse about two miles from the scene of our morning's exploits, and as it was near sunset we made our preparations for a quiet night's rest.

May 7th — Before sunrise this morning Gen. Stuart was in the saddle, and moving back to that same skirmish ground, which seemed to us all to possess an undue fascination for him, a feeling which none of us was disposed to share with him.

Genl. [Colonel Walter H.] Stevens, Chief Engineer of the Army, a stout, well-built and very military-looking officer, accompanied us.[39] Only a few couriers followed Gen. Stuart, as he intended to reconnoitre the enemy. We descended into the "hollow" without meeting any of their pickets, and obtained a good view of their lines. After spending an hour or so in this way, and no movement being made, we returned to our bivouac and spent the morning quietly. Reports from Genl. Fitz Lee came during the forenoon representing his command as heavily engaged with enemy's cavalry near Todd's Tavern, but gave cheering account of the way the men behaved, holding their ground in spite of all their attacks. Towards evening Gen. Gordon's Brigade, a fine, large fresh command of North Carolinians strengthened by the addition of the 3rd North Carolina Cavalry arrived and took position on the Catharpin Road. The enemy had had a small force, one brigade, on this road all day, but had barricaded the road very heavily in their front, as if expecting us to make the attack.

I was sent with one courier, Charles Lowndes, to inquire of Gen. Gordon the situation of affairs on this road.[40] I found Gen. Gordon just about sending forward a skirmish line to feel the enemy, and knowing that the best way to get the information Gen. Stuart wanted was to go and see for myself, I accompanied their advance. We moved cautiously forward across some open fields and then into a skirt of woods, where a momentary stir was created along the line by encountering a scouting party of our men & exchanging some shots with them, fortunately without damage to anybody. Pushing ahead of our line, I rode with Lowndes towards the enemy's first barricade. As we approached it, two Yankee cavalrymen rode away from behind it and retreated slowly down the road. We then rode up to the barricade and were peeping thro' it when all at once two loud reports startled us, and at the same instant two shells passed overhead a few feet above the barricade, and went hurtling up the road, passing over an entire regiment which was marching at a walk towards the barricade, and dropping harmlessly at the rear of the column. The regiment was immediately withdrawn to one side of the road, and dismounting, prepared to fight on foot. Gen. Gordon soon arrived on the ground, and sending forward his line, soon became hotly engaged. I then rode back to Gen. Stuart and told him what was going on. He waited until near sunset, and then taking a portion of Rosser's Brigade, moved over to Gordon's left flank. The men went in with a rousing cheer and drove back the enemy's right a short distance, but darkness coming on they were prevented from doing him much damage.

Gordon's men had fought well, driving them back about a mile from where they first commenced the fight.

I was sent along the line after dark with an order to Gen. Gordon to withdraw quietly and move back to camp near Shady Grove Church. After delivering the order I rode back along the skirmish line and repeated it to some of Gordon's Colonels, speaking in a low voice and cautioning the men to come off quietly as the lines were so close together that any conversation in the ordinary tone could have been distinctly heard. But in spite of my instructions, one old "Tar-heel," in the exuberance of his spirits, perched himself on a pine stump and clapping his arms to his sides in imitation of the lord of the barnyard, uttered a loud, clear crow, which however came near terminating fatally, for at the very same instant a Yankee fired in the direction of the noise, the bullet passing just in front of my horse and striking the stump on which our "chicken" was sitting. That shut him up effectually, and he "rolled off his log" amid the laughter of his comrades. As we came out, the men exchanged alternate "cheers" and "groans" with the Yankees, and the two lines chaffed each other considerably, calling one another names neither euphonious nor endearing.

Bivouacked that night not far from Shady Grove Church, and on Sunday morning, May 8th, we were in the saddle by day-light, and marching in the direction of Spotsylvania Court House The enemy was reported moving on that place, and two Divisions of Longstreet's Corps were pressing on to reach it before them. Gen. Stuart, accompanied only by his staff and a few couriers, struck off across country without regard to roads or by-paths, and we soon found ourselves going at a gallop along an unfrequented way, & suddenly debouching into an open field, saw that we were on the flank of a skirmish line of Infantry which we supposed to be our own. They let us approach within two or three hundred yards and then commenced firing on us in the most unprovoked manner. Fortunately for us there was a small piece of woods on our right, which we gained before they had time to do us any damage. In going thro' this piece of woods my horse plunged both his fore-feet into a stump-hole, filled with dry leaves, and fell, catching my left leg under him & bruising me badly. I had to lay there under him until he struggled to his feet, and then ascertaining that no bones were broken, I remounted and pushed on after our party. Found Gen. Stuart with a column of our Infantry, and heard him administer a pretty sharp rebuke to the skirmishers who had fired upon us without taking the time to ascertain who we were.

Pressing on as rapidly as possible, we passed the Infantry, and arrived at the Block House just in time to prevent the enemy from seizing that road. Gen. [Major General Richard H.] Anderson surrendered the command of the field to Gen. Stuart, and he, putting the line in order pushed forward the Division which was then on the ground, occupying a position on the edge of a corn-field over which the enemy were about to advance.

Gen. Fitz Lee, with the main body of his Division of Cav., had been opposing the advance of the 5th Corps U.S.A. all the morning. His men had fought most gallantly only yielding their ground when the swarming masses of Yankee Infantry had flanked them on both sides and threatened to capture the whole command.

It was here that Major James Breathed performed one of his most daring feats, which can best be described in the language of Gen. Fitz Lee who witnessed it. "Major Jas. Breathed by my order, placed a single gun in position on a little knoll, as we were falling back disputing the enemy's advance towards Spotsylvania Court House, etc, etc. (See "Old Dominion" for Jan. 1871. pp. 43-44.)[41]

The anticipated attack on our Infantry line was made about 12 o'clock, and at one time it seemed that the enemy would gain the day. Our men were lying behind rail-piles, and small hastily built earthworks; the enemy charged with spirit and determination, actually leaping the works in some places and inflicting bayonet-wounds on the men who were defending them. They were finally forced to retire under a galling fire, which strewed the corn-field with dead and wounded. I well remember the agonizing groans and painful contortions of some of these poor fellows as they lay in the hot sun between the two skirmish lines, out of the reach of friend or foe. {Side notation: See "Confederate Veteran" of August 1914 — Vol. XXII. No. 8 — for an account of this fight written by John Coxe — of Groveland, California. p. 356.}[42]

Re-inforcements were coming up every hour and by 5 o'clock P.M. our lines were strong enough to repel any attack which the force in hand in our front might choose to make. Sunday night was spent by Gen. Stuart & Staff at the Old <u>Block House</u>, in bivouac under some large oak trees on the roadside.

This was the last occasion, during our General's life-time, on which all our military family were together. We drank our coffee, smoked our pipes & turned in after the hard day's work without much of the light laughter & cheerful chit-chat which usually enlivened our camp-fires. Little did we dream however, that the morrow's dawn would lift the curtain of the saddest scene of all.

We were in the saddle bright and early on the morning of the 9th of May, and accompanied Genl. Stuart as he took his way very leisurely towards Spotsylvania Court House. Arriving there we halted, waiting to hear from Gen. Fitz Lee whose Division was on the Fredericksburg Road confronting the enemy as they prepared to move forward. During our halt, I went among the many wounded cavalrymen who were lying about on the court green, and found some old friends to whom I rendered some slight assistance, helping such as could leave get into ambulances, as the hospitals had been established further in our rear. Shepherd of the "Black Horse Troop" was here wounded & also Alexander Hunter.[43]

In a few minutes however, couriers came rapidly in reporting that Gen. Fitz Lee had commenced a skirmish with the enemy, who were in such heavy force that he doubted the possibility of maintaining his ground. Genl. Stuart immediately started to join him and when we reached our cavalry skirmish line, it was found almost useless to hold on in the face of such odds. A slow & leisurely retreat was begun, but strange to say, the enemy did not press us. Their shell flew wildly over-head, some of them bursting more than a mile in our rear. It occurred to many of us at the time, that the enemy here lost the best opportunity they had during the whole campaign, to fall upon our flank and destroy our army. The following statement will serve to show that there was on that morning some danger of such a disaster to our arms. While Genl. Stuart was skirmishing with the Enemy's advance on the Fredericksburg Road, he sent the writer of this to find the extreme right of our Infantry line, which was supposed by Genl. Stuart to be not very far from the road which Fitz Lee's Cav. were skirmishing. I hunted in vain at least a half hour, in which I must have ridden quite a mile in a straight line from the said Road, without finding a vidette or picket, or any human being who could tell me where our troops were. About the end of that time I accidently [sic] stumbled on a thin line of men, who were "digging dirt" very leisurely, and was informed by them that they were the right wing. They were on the extreme right of their brigade, ([Brigadier General Harry T.] Hay's La. Brigade, I think it was) and knew of no other troops near them. I saw the comd'g officer and was so informed.

I galloped back hastily to Genl. Stuart and reported accordingly. He at once rode off to find Genl. Lee, and I was soon after told that troops were moving to extend the line. If Gen. Grant could have known, and it seems to me that nothing could have been easier to ascertain, that his line overlapped ours for such an immense distance, it would have been the work of a very few minutes to move against our right flank, throw it into confusion and seize the very ground on which we held him at bay for more than a week.[44] It is probable tho' that no blame be attached to either commander. On our side, the dispositions of the previous evening were only temporary and made under a great emergency. Darkness coming rapidly on had put an end to anything

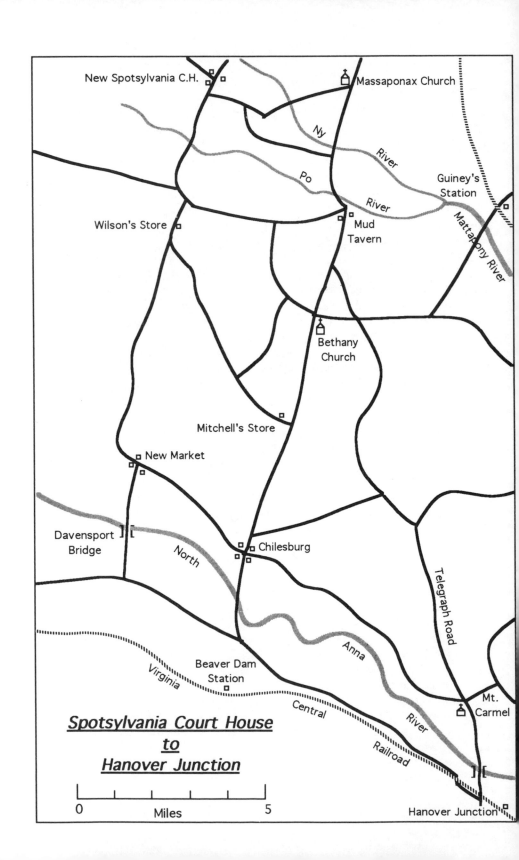

New Spotsylvania C.H.

Massaponax Church

Ny

River

Guiney's
Station

Po

River

Mattaponny River

Wilson's Store

Mud
Tavern

Bethany
Church

Mitchell's Store

New Market

Davensport
Bridge

North

Chilesburg

Telegraph Road

Anna

Mt.
Carmel

River

Beaver Dam
Station

Virginia

Central

Railroad

Spotsylvania Court House
to
Hanover Junction

Hanover Junction

0   Miles   5

like the formation of a regular line of battle. On the other side, it is most likely that Gen. Grant's masses were moving slowly, and the same causes had operated to prevent his discovery of the exact condition of our troops.

The whole forenoon of this day was spent in reconnoitring the enemy's position. There was an old church a short distance from Spotsylvania Court House near which Gen. Stuart and Gen. Lee remained for an hour or two. From the upper-windows of this church we could plainly see the enemy's wagon trains across the country, and occasionally detect the movement of small bodies of troops, especially artillery and cavalry.

It was at this church that Gen. Stuart received intelligence of the commencement of [Major General Philip H.] Sheridan's Raid upon Richmond. Information was brought during the morning that our pickets on the Telegraph Road had been driven in, and that a heavy force of the Enemy's Cavalry had passed down that road. Gen. Fitz Lee's Division was immediately withdrawn from the lines and hurried off in pursuit.

About 3 o'clock P.M. Gen. Stuart left the church & commenced that long & toilsome journey which terminated in his death. It might be worth while to dwell here for a moment on some sad thoughts which will rise in the mind in contemplation of the circumstances I am about to relate. He bade Gen. Lee "goodbye," and summoning a few of his staff officers, rode off from the Army. To a believer in the theory of "presentiments" it would have been easy to infer from Gen. Stuart's manner that he felt deeply and seriously the awful crisis that was at hand. The cheerful smile, the hearty laugh, the merry hum of his voice as he ran over and over some favorite song — "Her Bright Smile haunts me still," or "Ever of Thee I'm Fondly Dreaming" — one or the other of which he was continually humming, even in the midst of battle, all this was changed. His mind was at work with graver matters. Who can tell what the inner communings of his dauntless soul were then? It was on this very march that one of the men, our bugler, a man named Freed, who was riding just behind him remarked: "General, I believe you are happy in a fight." The General turned on him suddenly and said, "You're mistaken, Freed. I don't love bullets any better than you do. It is my duty to go where they are sometimes, but I don't expect to survive this war."[45]

After riding three or four miles, Gen. Stuart stopped at a very nice country residence, & rode in — Held a short conversation with the owner and two or three ladies who were on the porch, and then continued his march at a rapid gait, not drawing rein for nearly 16 miles. His old gray was a rapid traveller, trotting fast enough to keep our horses in a canter. I rode boot to boot with him all the way, and cannot remember hearing him say a word the whole time. At Mitchell's Store, not far from Chilesburg, we caught up with the rear of Fitz Lee's command. They had been skirmishing for some time with the enemy's rearguard, and firing was still going on, tho' it was too dark to continue it much longer.

Passing thro' some squads of dismounted men who had "come out" to look for their horses, one of them got in the way of the General's horse and came near being run over. Gen. Stuart reined up his horse to keep from hitting him and as the fellow jumped out of the road, he glanced up and caught sight of Stuart's hat & feather and recognizing it at once yelled out "Hurrah, boys! Here's old Jeb!" A long and loud shout followed this announcement, which seemed to infuse new life and energy into the tired and hungry troopers. Gen. Stuart not wishing to encourage this demonstration in the presence of the enemy, simply said to the soldiers around him as he rode on, "Don't holler, boys, until you get out of the woods."

Riding on Gen. Stuart found Genl. Fitz Lee near his skirmish line at the gate of a farm house, and a short conference took place between them. In another moment, he ordered the writer of this to return over the Road we had just traversed, until he met Gordon's Brigade, which had been ordered from the vicinity of Locust Grove and which had not reached Spotsylvania Court House when we left. Returning a distance of 5 or 6 miles I heard, as I neared Mud Tavern the noise of men & horses and soon found that it was the Brigade of Genl. Gordon. It was just going into camp, the Quartermaster having been ordered to provide corn & forage and luckily found a farmer in the neighborhood from whom he could obtain it. Dismounting I approached the house and inquiring for Gen. Gordon I was answered by that officer himself from the porch of a small house near the roadside. Making my way to him in the dark, he eagerly inquired after Stuart and I delivered my orders. "Gen. Stuart wants you to come right ahead, General," said I; to which Gordon replied, "By G__d, my men shall not move one foot till they feed up." He then said that it was out of the question to move his brigade until they had taken some rest. They had marched from Locust Grove since day break, over 40 miles, without stopping to feed or water, and then changing his tone, he kindly invited me to come and lie down by him on the porch. I did so, and in a few minutes we were both fast asleep. I was waked by Genl. Gordon, who had just ordered the brigade to move, and remounting we rode along together on our way to join Genl. Stuart. I remembered a point in the road where I had passed a picket, a man from the 4th Virginia Cavalry As we approached this picket I rode forward to notify him of the advance of the North Carolina Brigade and finding him on post, commenced talking with him. He pointed out to me the camp fire of his company which he said had been left there on duty, and as we stood there waiting for Gen. Gordon and his staff — a pistol flashed in the woods near the camp and the ball whistled over our heads — another and another shot came, & at least five or six shots were fired over our heads. We called out to the party firing, that we were friends, but even after that another bullet came. Gordon had arrived by this time and was intensely angry at the occurrence. We sent to the camp to know who it was that had done the firing, but learned that all were asleep there, & that none of the men were missing. This increased the mystery, and after waiting a few minutes without further hostile demonstration, we moved on, wondering at the strange occurrence, which to this day I have never been able to explain.[46]

We marched on without further incident and early that morning joined Gen. Stuart in the little village of Chilesburg. Here Stuart made his dispositions for the pursuit. Sending Gen. Fitz Lee's command on the direct road to Beaver Dam, he took Gordon's Brigade with him by another route crossing the Central Railroad further east.[47] He ordered me to accompany Gen. Fitz Lee's command, and I saw him no more that day until about 4 or 5 P.M. when the column assembled near Fork Church. I can therefore only say what occurred with the troops whom I accompanied. Leaving Chilesburg the 4th Virginia Cavalry, Col. Bob Randolph, in front, we crossed the North Anna River at a very bad ford, and pushed on towards the Railroad. As we neared the Station, we discovered that the woods & fences were burning, the Railroad torn up, and a body of the enemy standing in the road to dispute our approach. Col. Randolph was ordered to charge. In gallant style the order was obeyed, the leading squadron of the 4th Regiment going in and doing the work effectually. After a short & sharp contest the enemy broke and fled. We chased them several miles, capturing about twenty prisoners, some of whom poor fellows were infantry thus captured for the third time within a week — first by infantry in the Wilderness, & being sent on to Richmond had gotten as far as Beaver Dam when they were re-captured from their guards by Sheridan, and then again returned to captivity by the charge just spoken of. We learned from the prisoners, who belonged to the 3rd U.S. Regulars, that the Regular Brigade was the rear-guard and had been gone some hours, leaving their reg't behind to delay us.

Pushing on rapidly we arrived at Fork Church, and there halted to rest. Here Gen. Stuart came up, and turning our horses loose, to regale themselves on Major Price's sweet clover, we stretched ourselves on the soft grass, & bethought us of making a camp. Gen. Stuart had stretched himself out at full length on his back in the fresh rich clover and with his hat over his face was shading his eyes from the glare of the setting sun. I was lying by him. He turned to me and said, "I know where you want to be." "Yes," said I, "I expect you do." Well, go on," he replied, "and join me in the morning wherever you can find me." I needed no further orders, but mounting my tired horse rode off to my home in Hanover Co. which was only seven miles distant. Here I found my father, mother & family all well, and very much disturbed by the wild rumors of the enemy's approach. I was soon in bed & sound asleep, having first seen my horse stabled and plentifull [sic] fed. Early in the morning — May 11th 1864 — I started to find Gen. Stuart. He had bivouacked near

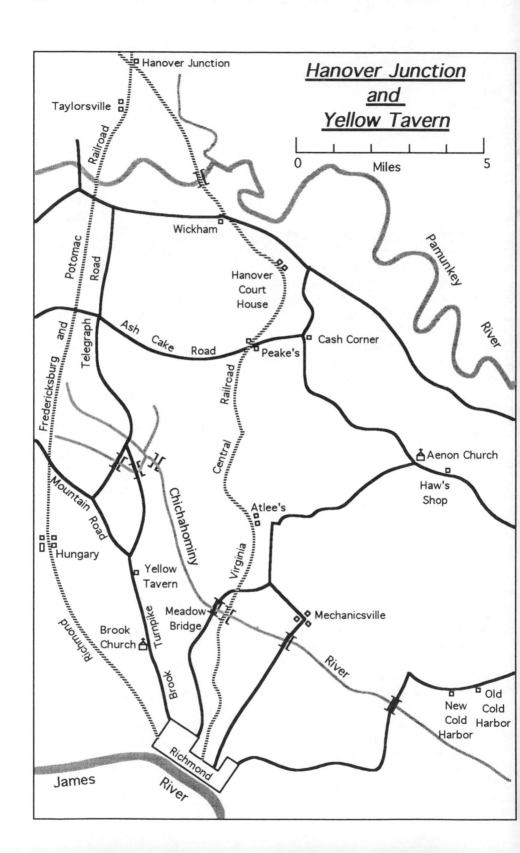

Taylorsville, but had broken camp & gone off towards Ashland before I could join him. Riding briskly forward I fell in with the rear guard of Wickham's brig'de and passing that command, caught up with Gen. Stuart at Ashland. Here a few moments before I arrived, a few prisoners had been caught — being some of a party sent by Sheridan to burn the depot and destroy the Railroad and telegraph at that Depot. They had succeeded in burning a few flat cars and setting fire to a large pile of cord wood alongside the Railroad — into which fire some heartless wag in our command was pretending, in all earnestness apparently, that he was ordered to pitch them. The prisoners evidently didn't relish the joke, their looks bespoke very decided fear that they would not stand the test quite as well as Shadrach, Meshac [sic]and Abednego,[48] for if anything could be hotter than a furnace seven times heated, it was the mass of blazing coals which was then before them.

Leaving Ashland we pushed on towards the Chickahominy River on the Telegraph Road. A few miles from Ashland Gen. Stuart received a message from Gen. Lomax, who had been sent with his brigade a considerable distance in advance of us to the effect that he was then at Yellow Tavern — no enemy in sight, and their whereabouts was unknown. The General then halted Wickham's brigade, and determined to await intelligence from his scouts — or from Gen. Gordon's brigade which had been left in the enemy's rear on the Mountain Road.

Becoming impatient of the delay, he called me to him and, giving me his field glasses, told me to go out on our flank in the direction of the Mountain Road — that I would find our vidette line out in that country — from which I should take two men as couriers — and that I must not return to him until I could send or bring him word exactly <u>where</u> the enemy was. I started at once on this duty, and had gotten about two miles from the telegraph road when I saw a cloud of dust a quarter of a mile or so across the country, and on inquiry, from the inmates of a cabin, learned that this was a party of Yankees who had been down to burn Dilly's Mill. The dust disappeared westward, and I turned to ride in the direction of the Mountain Road when I heard distinctly the sound of the guns at Yellow Tavern, showing that the enemy had turned up, just where we were expecting them.

Norfolk Virginia,
    53 Charlotte Street,
       February 28th 1894

Twenty years have passed since I penned the foregoing pages.

A life of busy professional work has prevented my return to this MS. and I find now that my memory, once so clear and reflective of the old war times and incidents, is sadly lacking now. Names and dates are fading away, and

I feel disinclined to continue the record of my experiences; old comrades have passed away, and the present generation seem incapable of giving any thoughtful consideration or appreciative attention to the struggles and sacrifices made by their fathers in their War for Independence.

But I have reached a point in the narrative, saddest of all to me, when I must chronicle the last hours of my dear General — the last great fight of General Stuart.

The sound of heavy firing reached me just as I was making my way towards the enemy's column then occupying the Mountain Road. I knew the country well enough to be able to locate the position of the respective heads of column, and I was sure they had come together at the junction of the Mountain Road with the Telegraph Road at the Yellow Tavern. Putting spurs to my horse I soon regained the Telegraph Road and turning south passed Wickham's Brigade marching on the road, slacking my pace as I caught up with Col. Bob Randolph at the head of the 4th Virginia. With him I recall a short conversation, each of us expressing our views briefly as to what was ahead of us, and I remember distinctly how surprised I was to find Col. Randolph, usually so bright and cheerful, and full of fight, now gloomy, depressed and apparently dispirited. I rallied him a little, but left him feeling that he was justified in being a little out of sorts this morning.

Pushing on I crossed the Bridge over the Chickahominy and soon reached Yellow Tavern. As I approached that place, a dropping fire between the skirmishers of Lomax's Brigade and a heavy line of dismounted cavalry of Sheridan's command was going on. General Stuart was on the spot, and as usual, among the skirmishers, directing their fire, and making his dispositions for the coming battle. I informed him that Wickham's brigade was still far behind; he had already sent for it, and if it could have reached him in time, with the wagons and ambulances, I have little doubt that he would have passed by the junction of the two roads, even under the enemy's fire, and then faced about, thus interposing our column between the Enemy and Richmond. But whether this became impossible, owing to the slow march of Wickham's Brigade, or because General Stuart desired to remain on Sheridan's left flank and so allowed him to get in front of us on the Richmond road (Brook Turnpike) certain it is that after a short skirmish, the enemy outflanking the left of Lomax's Brigade, got possession of Yellow Tavern, and we retired northward on the Telegraph Road. About a half mile north of Yellow Tavern a cut or depression in the road seemed to form a good defensive position and here Gen. Stuart ordered a stand to be made. At this point the 5th [Virginia] Cavalry, Col. H. [Colonel Henry] Clay Pate was assembling his men, all dismounted. Gen. Stuart had ordered up a battery — "The Baltimore Light Artillery" (I think it was) which we had picked up near Hanover Junction, and it had been put in position at the edge of a piece of woods on the west side of the Telegraph

Road, and was firing briskly on the lines which Sheridan was forming in the direction of the Mountain Road.[49] The moment I joined General Stuart at this Battery, he pointed to Pate's Reg't and said, "Go and tell Colonel Pate to hold that position at all hazards," emphasizing the three last words; whereupon I put my horse at his full speed and found Col. Pate among his men, dismounted, sword in hand, rallying them and awaiting the attack which in another moment burst upon him. I delivered the order in the very words I had received it, and I can see Col. Pate now as he stood, looking me square in the eye, with his cold grey eyes and pallid face, (not from fear for he was habitually pale) but uttering no response, and thinking he had not heard me, I leaned over on my horse closer to him, and spoke louder, repeating the order, "Colonel: General Stuart says hold this position at all hazards." Still no reply came from his lips, and he gave me no message to take back to Stuart; but I saw he had heard and understood my orders in their full significance, as a veritable "death-sentence." As the men of the 5th came pressing around him into the road, leaving their exposed positions in the open field west of it, I saw there was little to hope for from them. It was a trap and they knew it. They were flanked on the south, and the enemy in overwhelming numbers came crowding up firing into the group of men in the cut. I endeavored to make my way back to General Stuart but found that the Road by which I had reached Col. Pate was practically in the enemy's hands, as they were so close to it on the west side that they commanded every foot of it, and it was certain death to attempt to pass back that way.

The open field on the east side offered but little better hope of escape, but it was my only chance. Dashing into the growing wheat my horse thoroughly aroused to the exigency of the occasion seemed as eager to get away as his rider. A few plunges and I felt him swerve under me, & wheel suddenly to the left, with a loud snort, as he narrowly avoided going headlong into a wide and deep ditch. He flew along this ditch for a hundred yards, each instant getting nearer towards the enemy, and seeing that would never do, I determined to attempt the long jump. Thoroughly aroused he rose under me and cleared the yawning gulf, landing on the other side in safety — whence by a short circuit I rejoined my General in a very few minutes. He had witnessed the capture of Pate's men, and the fall of Col. Pate on the spot where I had just left him. {Side notation; Oct. 16/95}[50]

I have heard, since the war, that General Stuart and Colonel Pate, who had long been estranged, (on account of the proceedings of a courtmartial ordered by Gen. Stuart for the trial of Col. Pate) had, on that fatal day, made up their differences and for the first time in many months, shaken hands and tacitly agreed to forget the past. Of this I can recall nothing, but one of my brethren of the Staff has told me that he heard Stuart lament, in feeling words, the death of Pate, and say he died the death of a gallant soldier.[51]

Immediately on my return to the General's side, he gave me orders to General Wickham. These were to hasten in with Wickham's brigade on the extreme right of the line and to attack vigorously whatever was found in their front, the purpose being to demonstrate strongly on that flank with the view to making the enemy let go their hold on the Telegraph Road. I put my horse to his utmost speed to reach Genl. Wickham, and searched in vain for that officer, but making my way across country towards the firing on our right I reached the edge of a body of heavy timber and to my surprise found our whole line retiring. Meeting Captain Aleck Payne of the Black Horse Troop, 4th Va. Cav. trudging towards me I told him of my orders and asked if he had seen his Brigade Commander, or could he direct me to him. While talking to Capt. Payne, his man came dropping back into the open field, and Payne quietly told me it was impossible to advance against the heavy lines of dismounted men posted in the heavy timber, and whose fire he had stood as long as it was possible for any men to stand. He had ordered his men out and had sent word for re-inforcement. But the attack which he had just made had the desired effect — the enemy on the Telegraph Road, hearing the heavy firing had suddenly fallen back to their main lines, and relieved the pressure on our left.

As I stood with Captain Payne, taking in the situation on this part of the line, a courier rode up and handed me a dispatch addressed by General James B. Gordon to General Stuart, the poor fellow's horse was so exhausted that he begged me to carry it to Genl. Stuart. I told him to follow me out and I would carry him to the General. In a few minutes I rejoined Genl. Stuart at the spot where I left him, and delivered to him Gen. Gordon's dispatch. It simply announced his skirmish with the enemy's rearguard at Ground Squirrel Bridge, on the Mountain Road on the evening of the 10th, and I think mentioned in particular a gallant charge made by the 1st North Carolina Cavalry.

Stuart read the message, and slapping his right hand on his thigh, exclaimed, "Bully for Gordon!" and then in a little altered tone, said, sotto voce, "I wish he was here!"

The [2nd Maryland] Battery, near which Gen. Stuart kept his position during the greater part of the day, had been brought back into position as soon as the enemy left the Telegraph Road, and was dropping shell at intervals into the woods occupied by the Enemy. I told Gen. Stuart at once of the condition in which I had found Genl. Wickham's line, and that I had thought it best to let him know this; that I had not found Gen. Wickham and asked if I should go and search again.

He said no, it was too late now. He was in communication with Gen. Fitz Lee and had sent him orders as to that part of the line. Then turning to me he said, "Our ammunition is exhausted." "Our wagons have not been able to keep up." "I want you to go to Richmond, taking a detail of 20 men, and bring back all the cartridges you can carry." "First, go to that house yonder" — pointing to Crenshaw's house, which stood on an elevation beyond a deep ravine in our rear. "Get all the information you can as to the by-paths through the farms between this place and Richmond." "Be careful to keep off the Telegraph Road until you are well behind the enemy's flankers — and return to me as fast as you can!" "After you have gotten directions as to the route from Crenshaw's house, return to me and I will give you 20 men and orders for the ammunition!"

Leaving Genl. Stuart at the Battery, I crossed the Telegraph Road, and descended into the ravine. It was with great difficulty that I made my way through, climbing the steep sides of the cliffs on the opposite side, and emerging into the farm near the dwelling-house. There I found a number of wounded men, attended by surgeons, and soon had the owner of the place and obtained from him minute description of the paths leading across the Brook. Beyond that, and into Brook Hill, I knew the way well. So making a memorandum in my little Order-Book, I started back to General Stuart.

January 4th 1902 All my good resolutions have been broken, & I am astonished to find that the last few pages of this memoir were written as long ago as October 16th 1895! I take up the story where I left off

Leaving Crenshaw's house, I took the road leading out towards the Telegraph Road, and in a few minutes met Genl. Lomax and his Aid-de-Camp [sic], my cousin, Lieut. James Hunter, Jr.

They asked me if I had seen Col. Pate, and then told me that his dead body was lying on the floor of a small farm house where we met. At Gen. Lomax's suggestion, I dismounted and entered the house to pay my last tribute of respect to Col. Pate whose untimely death grieved Genl. Lomax deeply. As no firing was then going on, I did not feel that I was losing any time or neglecting my duty by stopping a moment to view Col. Pate's body and note the fatal wound — full in the forehead — which had caused instant death at the very moment I rode away from him as the enemy closed in on him. I spent not more than five minutes in this sad mission, but that space of time may have made a serious difference in my fate that day. Mounting our horses, Genl. Lomax, Lt. Hunter and I rode together slowly towards the Main Road; reaching it I turned to the left in the direction of the battery where I had parted with Gen. Stuart; Gen. Lomax and his Aide turned to the right and went towards the River, where a part of Lomax's Brigade was held in reserve. Riding on towards the battery, I passed an opening in the woods and obtained a view obliquely across the battle-field. From a point of woods near the enemy's lines I saw a Squadron of their Cavalry move out at a trot, followed by another and another, until nearly a regiment was in view. Instantly I wheeled my horse, galloped back and called loudly to Gen. Lomax who heard me, as I yelled out to him, "General, they are charging our Battery." He understood me at once, and put spurs to his horse, and in a minute I saw him coming back towards me leading a Squadron of the Sixth Virginia, all coming at speed. As he reached me, all hands drew sabre and started with increased speed to reach the battery, if possible, at the same moment with the enemy; Gen. Lomax, Hunter and myself, riding abreast, were in advance of our squadron and had reached a point in the Road where it passes through a cut, and descends sharply to a little stream, the opposite side being steeper, if anything, than the side on which we were approaching. But just as the Squadron was descending the grade I saw coming down the opposite slope one gun of our Battery which had escaped capture and whose drivers with two or three men were plunging madly down the narrow road; the inevitable happened. The horses under whip & spur, frantic with excitement rushed into us, throwing men & horses to each side of the road and breaking up all our hopes of a counter-charge upon the enemy. Inextricable confusion followed; it was simply impossible for Gen. Lomax or the officers of the Squadron to remedy the disaster, that gun had plunged through us from front to rear, and no time to form again was allowed; the enemy's horsemen were in among the other three guns, busy with their capture, and seemed to me in great confusion. A well-ordered and sudden charge, such as we had expected to deliver, would have staggered them and prevented them from carrying off the guns. But, alas, our own escaped gun had played the mischief. Our dismounted skirmishers then commenced falling back, many a fellow calling loudly for cartridges, having fired his last shot. I stood for some minutes at the spot where our squadron had been broken up — nearly every man gone, and could see the enemy crowding the ridge in front of me, and was soon the recipient of their attentions, bullet after bullet striking near me and under my horse. I was waiting & expecting every moment to see Genl. Stuart appear, so sure was I that he would ride out of the melee', as I had so often seen him do, smiling and unharmed. But no, the enemy had possession of the road and all our men seemed to have abandoned it. I could not see what was taking place towards the right or west side of the Road, but the fight was well over and the enemy, both mounted and dismounted were uncomfortably near. Riding slowly back about a hundred yards, I was surprised to meet Lieut. William Hoxton, of the Horse Artillery, who was bringing up one of his guns, and asked me where he could get into good position to open on them.[52] I told him as plainly as I could that there was no use and no place there for a gun; there was nothing at that moment between his gun and the enemy, and that unless he wanted to lose his piece, he had better retire it to the River. Hoxton was a good soldier, brave to a fault, and handsome as he was brave. He was one of two men, Edwin Sully being the other, who had brained a Yankee with sponge-staff at

Brandy Station — June 9th 1863. He looked at me reproachfully and urged me to show him a place and point out the Yankees. I told him to follow me, and we rode together towards the enemy. He saw the situation at a glance, and then agreed to retire the gun. We came off the ground together, and soon reached the Bridge where the Telegraph Road crosses the Chickahominy River. There I found many men assembling, but in great disorder. Major McClellan met me and told me that Gen. Stuart had been wounded, and added "his body is in the enemy's hands" — "we must go after him." He wanted a few volunteers with good horses who would join us in a charge upon the enemy and penetrate to the point where Gen. Stuart was supposed to be. I set to work at once to secure men for this "forlorn hope." I stated the terms on which they were to volunteer and in a few minutes had several with me, tho' I did not know one of them personally.

{Side notation: Got into ambulance and leaned over him asking him to tell me how he had been wounded; he gave me a brief account of it — as follows:}

I reported to Maj. McClellan with them and we were about to start for the work, when he informed me that Gen. Stuart had been brought off the field and was then in an ambulance on Gen. Fitz Lee's line. We rode forward and in a few minutes met the ambulance, and at my first glance into Genl. Stuart's face I saw that he was severely wounded and suffering great pain. With the ambulance were Dr. Fontaine, our Chief Surgeon, Major Venable, and old Carpenter, a courier, and joining them we turned east, leaving the Telegraph Road & crossing the river at another bridge.[53] Driving on rapidly, we encountered a heavy storm, thunder, lightning and pouring torrents of rain. When we reached Atlee's Station, on the Virginia Central Railroad the ambulance was halted under a huge oak tree, and here Dr. Fontaine urged the General to take a dose of whiskey from a canteen which Doctor Archie Randolph had given us as we left the field.[54] The General resisted, but Dr. Fontaine prevailed upon him to swallow it, and this was the first and only drop of whiskey that passed Stuart's lips in all his life.

Driving on we overtook Doctor L_____ [name unknown], who resided at Mechanicsville, and as soon as he learned that Gen. Stuart was in the ambulance, quickened his speed, & rode on ahead to have some hot coffee made for the General by the time we could arrive there. The coffee was brought out to the gate, with some beautiful hot biscuit, but after tasting his cup slowly, the General put it aside, unable to take what had always been to him the greatest comfort.

Here I left the ambulance, and putting my tired horse to his best trot, hastened on to Richmond to report to Gen. Braxton Bragg the events of the day, the serious wounding of Genl. Stuart and to have a bed prepared for the General immediately on his arrival. I reached Richmond about 10 o'clock at night and hastened to Dr. [Charles] Brewer's house; the Doctor was a brother-in-law of Gen. Stuart, having married Mrs. Stuart's sister — and there a room and bed were prepared for him.

I then rode to Genl. Bragg's office. Ushered into that officer's presence, I made my report, as briefly as possible, my mind chiefly occupied with the thought of my wounded General. I never met with a colder reception. For all I could see, the loss of Genl. Stuart was to General Bragg a matter of supreme indifference; he expressed no sympathy, either by word or in manner, and he indicated no interest in me or my message. He sent no message back by me to Stuart, and I confess I was not loth to leave the presence of his cold-blooded Highness.

Incessant riding — with little food — from May 4th to 11th passing through fatigues and exposure and the chance of repeated battles had worn me out, and my poor horse also. I cannot recall where I spent the balance of that sad night, but I think it was at the hospitable home of my dear friends — Rev. Joshua Peterkin and family. There I remember meeting again Dr. Thomas H. Williams and Mrs. Williams, and Miss Ellen Beall — what happy days I used to spend with them in 1862!

The morning of 12th May, 1864, dawned dull & cloudy, and rain fell all the morning. At Dr. Brewer's all was care and anxiety. I could not bring myself to believe that the General's wound was mortal, and not until Dr. John Fontaine assured me that there was no hope for his recovery did I force myself to contemplate the extent of our loss. Personally my grief was as great as if my own father was dying, while the disaster to our cause and the calamity to the Army was, in my judgment, irreparable.

About 1 o'clock p.m. I was sitting by the General's bedside, holding his left hand in mine, when suddenly a loud shouting and noise in the street, Broad Street, was heard. Gen. Stuart opened his eyes, and in an excited voice exclaimed, "What's that?" "Go and see!" I left him and hurried over to Broad Street; an ambulance had just passed going east, and around it was a motley crowd, some of them shouting & cheering. Asking what was the matter, I was told: "They have a Yankee General in that ambulance — a prisoner captured today out on the Brook Turnpike." I did not believe it, but went back and found Genl. Stuart in a doze and did not disturb him with the news.

It turned out that the rumor thus circulated was sadly distorted, for in truth there was a General in that ambulance, but it was none other that [sic] our own dear commander of the North Carolina Brigade — Brig. General James B. Gordon, wounded that morning near Brook Hill, and brought to the Hospital on 12th Street, where he died only a few days after Stuart.

My last ride with Gordon was on the night of the 9th when I was bringing him up to Chilesburg. He was a fine soldier, brave and true, and much beloved and admired by Gen. Stuart.

I remained at Stuart's bedside until about 3 p.m. when I went to dine at Mr. Rutherford's, by invitation of my friend Miss Emily. When I returned to the house, Dr. Brewer's, the general was slowly sinking and at or near 8 p.m. May 12th 1864, he breathed his last. Mrs. Stuart arrived from Col. Fontaine's, in Hanover County, just a few minutes after he died. The next morning, I visited in person the several General Officers whom I invited to act as pall-bearers, among them Gen. [Brigadier General] Joseph R. Anderson, who is the only one I now recall as being one of them. I cannot now say positively whether the funeral took place on the 13th of May, or the 14th, certainly not later than the 14th. It was a dull, dark gloomy day & rainy. The interment took place in Hollywood Cemetery, and all that was mortal of the best soldier I ever knew rests there.[55]

The next morning, the members of Gen. Stuart's Staff hastened to leave Richmond on our return to duty with the Army. I think those in our little party were: Major A.R. Venable, Major McClellan, Surgeon John B. Fontaine, with couriers Carpenter, Ellis, Thompson and one or two others.[56] We reached "Dundee" that night, Dr. Price's hospitable home, near Hanover Court House and there spent the night. The sympathy and sorrow of this whole family was expressed in the kindest manner, for Gen. Stuart had always been a dear friend to every member of it.

The next day we pushed on, and by a long hard march reached the Army, then facing Grant's hosts in the lines at Spotsylvania Court House Major McClellan reported our arrival at Genl. R.E. Lee's Hdqrs, and orders were promptly issued assigning each one of the Staff, except myself, to duty in some direction. McClellan & Venable to Hampton's Staff, etc. etc. But it was the law of the War Dept. at that time that an Aid-de-Camp [sic], upon the death of his General, lost his commission, and there was no further use for him as an officer. This being so, my duty was clear, and I determined to seek my old Company, "F," in the 9th Virginia Cavalry and re-enlist as a private. A few days furlough was given me, and taking with me my friend, William R. Berkeley, of Farmville, Va., who had been a field-officer early in the war, but was then a courier at Hdqrs. Cav. Corps, I started for home in Hanover, riding my horse "Brandy" and leading my old Yankee cob, or rather, letting my negro boy "Henry" ride the cob.

We reached Cedar Hill that night, and were welcomed by my father, mother, sister & uncle, and there settled down to rest. But contrary to this hope, the troops were soon upon us. In a few days Hanover Junction was the scene of active preparation for battle. The Army rapidly assembled and stretched its lines north and westward towards Jericho — and southeastward through our plantation, digging light breastworks all along our front. Genl. [Major General Jubal] Early made his Hdqrs. at Cedar Hill, my home, and his line of battle ran clear across our wheatfield {Side notation: then in fine condition and promising a good crop which was nearly all destroyed by the troops} just a few hundred yards north of the Virginia Central Railroad track. My father & uncle remained at home, but my mother and sister were sent to Richmond, as we daily expected the attack of Grant's troops. No fighting occurred however, except one evening away off on the left near Jericho. On or about the 25th May 1864, my brother Jim and I set off from Cedar Hill having learned that all the troops of the Army of Northern Virginia had disappeared or were fast falling back towards Richmond. We marched to Ashland, or its vicinity, and reached Atlee's Station on the 27th. There I saw Gen. Lee's ambulance pass, the General himself in it, and unable to mount his horse, on account of some temporary illness.[57] Towards nightfall the sound of firing induced me to push on to Haw's Shop, where I found the Cavalry just coming out of what had proved to be a rather severe engagement. I passed through some new troops, Millen's Georgia Battalion, and found them lamenting the loss of many of their brave men, among them I think their Major or Commanding officer.[58] This was their first fight, and they suffered heavily.

As I rode on in the twilight I passed a column of horsemen, and heard my name called out by one of them. Turning I recognized my friend, Robert E. Lee, Jr., who shook hands with me, and just then his brother Maj. Genl. W.H.F. [Major General William Henry Fitzhugh, "Rooney"] Lee called out, "Bob, who is that?" Bob answered: "The Garnett." "Tell him to ride up here," said the General, and I did so. For some miles I rode beside Genl. Rooney Lee, whose acquaintance I had made on his return from prison, and I had shared my tent with him at Genl. Stuart's Headquarters during a visit he had paid us in winter quarters near Orange Courthouse. Perhaps his recollection of my hospitality induced him to ask me to spend the night with him and we went into bivouac on the road not far from Atlee's Station. He asked me what I was doing. I told him I was going back to my old company in the 9th Virginia Cavalry, but that just at that moment I was looking for Genl. Wickham, having received an indirect message to the effect that Gen. Wickham wanted my services at his Hdqrs. Gen'l Lee very promptly said, "You had better stay with me; you know all my staff, and you will be welcome here." Said I: "General, I thank you very much, nothing would be more agreeable to me, but my commission has expired, and I must go back to the ranks of my Company." He said, "No that will never do; I will write a letter to the Secretary of War at once, asking that you be commissioned and assigned to duty on my staff with your same rank."

He did so that night in bivouac, and by daylight I was riding to Richmond. Arriving there, I sought my uncle, Hon. S.R. Mallory, Secretary of the Navy, who went immediately to the Secretary of War, and in less than an hour my commission was signed and in my pocket. The next day I was back at Genl. Rooney Lee's side, and engaged with him in the fight at Ashland with Wilson's Cavalry, June 1st 1864.

"Blame me not, O Reader, for the subjects are
numberless and my memory is weak, and I
write at long intervals in different years."

— Leonardo da Vinci

March 7th 1903

Norfolk, Virginia December 5th 1912

It was this accidental meeting with Capt. Robert E. Lee, Jr., and his brother, that made me a staff officer of Major General Wm.H.F. Lee, with whom I served from that date up to the first week in March 1865, when I was promoted to the rank of Captain and Assistant Adjutant General on the Staff of Brigadier General William P. Roberts, who was then placed in command of [Brigadier General James] Dearing's old Brigade of W.H.F. Lee's Division.

Of Gen'l Roberts and his little Brigade I will have much to say — if this memoir is ever completed.

General Wm.H.F. Lee, on the 1st June 1864, commanded two Brigades — (1) Chambliss' Brigade, composed of the 9th, 10th and 13th Virginia Cavalry, and (2) the North Carolina Brigade, formerly Gordon's Brigade, afterwards known as Barringer's Brigade, now composed of the 1st, 2nd, 3rd and 5th North Carolina Cavalry.

It was not until we reached Petersburg that Dearing's Brigade was assigned to W.H.F. Lee's Division.

My association with Gen. "Rooney" Lee was from the first always of the most pleasant character. My appointment on his Staff at his own request was most unexpected as well as flattering, and I soon made friends of his whole military family, whose names were as follows:

L. Tiernan Brien, Major and A.A. Genl.
John M. Lee, Major and Inspector Genl.
James S. Gilliam, Chief Surgeon
Joseph Walters, Capt. & A.Q.M.
Frank S. Robertson, Lieut. & Engineer Officer
Thomas W. Pierce, Capt. & Ord. Officer
Robert E. Lee, Jr., Lieut. & A.D.C.
Beverly B. Turner, Lieut. & A.D.C.
Philip P. Dandridge, Lieut. & A.D.C.[59]

The name of the Division Commissary has escaped my memory, and there may have been others whose names should appear in the list.

LIEUTENANT FRANK SMITH ROBERTSON
Courtesy of Mrs. Sally Bruce B. McClatchey

I was assigned as Aid-de-Camp [*sic*], but was also made to perform the duties of Provost Marshal of the Division, whenever such disagreeable service was required. After serving with Gen. Lee as actively as I could all day through many long marches, skirmishes and battles, it was no pleasant duty to have to take charge at night of large numbers of prisoners and march many miles to deliver them over to Major [David B.] Bridgford, the Provost Marshal of the Army.

But coming as I did from General J.E.B. Stuart's Staff, a comparative stranger and the last man on the list of the Division Staff, it was natural that such duty should fall on me, and I never complained about it, on the principle perhaps of "the last man in bed must put out the light."

But to return to the fight at Ashland: Lee's Division had been hotly engaged with the Enemy's Cavalry on the 31st May at Hanover Court House and had retired at dusk to the vicinity of Wickham's, having been rather roughly handled.

I remember the loss of Lieut. [Lieutenant Charles Edward] Ford of the Horse Artillery who was killed that evening, and was buried on the road-side as we retired.[60]

The morning of the 1st June found us drawn up, mounted and in line, on the high ground just south of Wickham's, an excellent position to meet the advancing enemy. Their long blue lines, both mounted and dismounted stretched entirely across the level meadows and wheatfields of Wickham's fine plantation. Anticipating their attack on our front with every advantage in our favor I was hopeful of an easy repulse. They seemed to be in no hurry to begin the fight and we waited patiently for them to open the ball. I was sitting my horse near Genl. Lee, watching the splendid pageant of ever-increasing numbers of blue horsemen, fully displayed to our view in the plains below, when one of our scouts rode up and told the General that the enemy were moving a heavy column around our right-flank, then very much exposed and easily turned. In a few minutes Gen. Lee ordered his Division to retire upon Ashland, leaving Gen. [Brigadier General] Bradley T. Johnson to retire on the Court House road with two pieces of Artillery, but to dispute the enemy's advance and delay them as far as possible.

This Gen. Johnson did as well as he could, but the enemy pressed him severely, and he lost several of his Maryland Regiment, among them the brave Colonel [Lieutenant Colonel] Ridgely Brown, who fell in a charge on that road.

Genl. Lee halted his Division just east of Ashland and rested at ease, the enemy not appearing to have followed us. But the General appeared somewhat solicitous about Genl. Johnson's command, who were resisting the enemy on the upper road, and turning to me he ordered me to take one squadron from the 3rd North Carolina Cavalry and move rapidly to Gen. Johnson's aid. When I went to get the Squadron from the 3rd North Carolina, Major [Roger] Moore who was in command of that Regiment, demurred and requested me to say to Gen. Lee that he would like to accompany the squadron if it was to be sent away under my command. I told him there was no time to lose but I would be glad to have him ride with me — so we started at a rapid gait northward on the Old Telegraph Road, and soon reached the point where Gen. Bradley Johnson was fighting, just at the crossing of the County road and the Richmond, Fredericksburg & Potomac Railroad. Here I met Gen. Johnson, delivered my message to him from Gen. Lee, with his compliments, and pointing him to the squadron just behind me, said that it was sent by Gen. Lee to his assistance.

Gen. Johnson, rather brusquely I thought, exclaimed:"I don't want your Squadron — Take it back," — "Col. Brown has just been killed" — I cannot stop the enemy here," — "I am now falling back across the Railroad." Surprised at this reception and at Gen. Johnson's refusal of the Squadron, I turned to Major Moore, who had heard Gen. Johnson's order, and said, "Major, we must get back to Gen. Lee just as fast as possible — Go at a gallop," and turning away from the Maryland regiment who were then moving back, we took the road back to Ashland. As we neared the Ash-cake road I heard firing, and pushing ahead at a run, we crossed that road just as the head of the enemy's column appeared on our left coming at a charge, and the rear of our Squadron swept across their front within pistol shot. But neither party fired a shot, doubtless their surprise was as great as ours, tho' I had been expecting just what happened. Immediately after crossing their front we rode into our own lines, which had been moved from our starting point and were then on the Telegraph Road, and facing north towards Ashland.

Major Moore and his Squadron found his Regiment and I rejoined Genl. Lee on the Telegraph Road.

Here a message came from Genl. Wade Hampton stating that he, with Rosser and Young, was in the enemy's rear, driving them through Ashland, having captured some of their "led-horses" and that the enemy were in considerable disorder. This was almost immediately followed by an order to Gen. Lee to attack at once. I saw now how unfortunate it was that we had opened the gate and let the enemy pass through into Ashland. Of course Gen. Lee was not to blame, as he had no idea that Gen. Hampton was attacking the enemy's rear. If he had only been informed of that fact he would never have uncovered Ashland, and I have always thought that we lost here the only opportunity I ever saw for destroying a whole Division of Yankee Cavalry in fifteen minutes. As it happened, we had to change front, and swing around to the road leading into Ashland. The enemy had gotten into Ashland before us, and facing about were ready to repel our attack. Gen. Lee promptly obeyed Gen. Hampton's order, and sent me to lead the 5th North Carolina Cavalry. Taking the Regiment in column of fours, dismounted, I pushed with them across Rosser's front, meeting Gen. Rosser and Lieut. Richard C. Marshall of his staff just as I crossed the road leading into Ashland.

Just at this moment the sound and smoke of battle was heavy, deafening and blinding, but I saw coming out of the line on the Telegraph Road an officer, supported by two others, on his horse, shot through the breast and bleeding profusely, whom I recognized as my very gallant old friend, Genl. P.M.B. Young, of Georgia.

Calling to the men behind me to face to the front as they crossed the road, I yelled at Gen. Rosser: "Where shall we go in?" Pointing to the right he yelled back — "There, in there!"

Pushing my horse among them on the right of the line, several shells from the enemy's battery close up in front passed over my head, cutting limbs from the trees one of which fell across my horse's rump and came near dragging me out of the saddle. As we reached the telegraph road, the west side of which was thickly set with heavy undergrowth of bushes and brush, a Sergeant of the 5th, named Tillett with twelve of his Company pushed through this thicket and as they reached the far side, they delivered their fire point-blank upon a battery of the enemy's Horse Artillery in the open field and only a few yards from the thicket. Sergeant Tillett told me that just as they fired, a line of Yankee skirmishers rose out of a ditch and killed every man of Tillett's Company, he alone escaping their fire.

Sergeant Tillett, of the 5th North Carolina, became a very remarkable part of my army life after this. He was a brave and intelligent scout and soldier. He seemed to have leave to absent himself from his regiment when a fight was either imminent or actually going on, and he was always finding out what the enemy were doing or attempting to do. Whenever he met me he would always suggest some plan to ascertain the enemy's movements, and he seemed to be often on the lookout for me. I will have occasion to mention him more than once in this account of Army service.

But to proceed with the Ashland affair: — After some further firing, this Battery was hastily withdrawn and the whole line of the enemy rapidly retired through Ashland. As we went forward I rode with Lt. Col. [Lieutenant Colonel] Robert A. Caskie, of the 10th Virginia Cavalry. Pointing to three dead

Yankees lying at considerable distances apart but in the same general direction, on the level green sward stretching east of the village, Col. Caskie said: "Those are the three best shots I have seen during the whole war; one of my men killed those three Yankees while they were running, without missing a shot."

{Side notation: See So. Hist. Papers Vol VII p. 292 for Gen. RE Lee's report of this Ashland affair.}

May 5th 1913 —

Pushing on through Ashland we found the enemy's rear guard retiring northward along the Railroad, and they were soon out of our sight, retreating rapidly until they reached the road to Wickham's, the very spot at which I had led the Squadron of the 3rd North Carolina Cavalry to Gen. Johnson's assistance, and which he had so ungraciously refused. The whole of Wilson's Cavalry Division here made good their retreat towards Wickham's and the Court House, having succeeded in burning the Railroad Bridge over the South Anna River after driving Gen. Johnson's and the Maryland Cavalry from their front.

The whole affair was badly managed on our part, and what should have been a great victory for us must be numbered among the "lost opportunities."

Wm.H.F. Lee's Division bivouacked South of Ashland — Hampton's Division moved towards Atlee's — or spent the night on the road. On the 2nd June our Division joined Hampton's near Atlee's Station and camped for the night. On the 3rd both Divisions moved at sunrise and marched to Haw's Shop where we found a body of Grant's Infantry occupying the heavy works they had put there a few days before. We attacked them rather feebly — and developed a force of infantry too strongly posted for serious battle. And in the course of an hour or so of skirmishing, I was pleased to hear Gen. Hampton give the order to withdraw. Before leaving I was told that a wounded Confederate was lying in a house at Haw's Shop. I had heard a few days before that my friend and cousin St. George T. Brooke, of the 2nd Virginia Cavalry, Wickham's Brigade had been severely wounded in the fight here on the 28th May — just a week ago. Entering the house I found Brooke painfully shot and lying on a rough bed, being nursed by the kind women who lived in this very humble abode. I had only time to shake hands with him, and promise him to let his family in Richmond know where to find him, which was done and he was safely removed to Richmond. He survived the war, and became a learned Professor of Law in the University of West Virginia, and is today living at Charlestown, West Virginia.

The enemy's skirmishers drove me out of Haw's Shop and riding with Major Venable (Andrew R.) I ascended a steep little hill to get a better view of them. Just as we reached the crest we were fired on by several of them, and beat a hasty retreat down a rocky and very steep slope. Reaching the foot of the hill, and thinking I had heard the stroke of a bullet, I turned to Maj. Venable and asked if he was hit. "I think not," he said, "Are you?" He wore a heavy frock coat the tails of which had been pressed thick by the sagging of his sabre-belt. To this fortunate accident he owed his life. A bullet had struck him just above the cantle of his saddle — a posteriori, so to speak, going through the thick folds of his coat tails piercing every garment he had on; he found it in the seat of his drawers and withdrew it rather triumphantly and with great satisfaction that it had gone no further.

We rejoined our retiring column and marched back to the vicinity of Meadow Bridge where we encamped for two or three days. During our rest here, I got leave one afternoon to pay a visit to my friends — the family of Mr. John Stewart, at Brookhill. I was riding a fine bay stallion belonging to Lt. Robert E. Lee, Jr. — a fiery animal and so restive that when I arrived at the iron gate leading in to Brookhill and attempted to open the gate, the horse bolted in before I could fairly get him past the sharp iron spear-heads on the gate, and I received a gash on my right knee, the scar of which remains to this day. Miss Mary kindly brought needle & thread and mended the rent trousers and relieved my embarrassment at appearing in the parlor all "tattered and torn."

Riding back to our camp I turned in late that night with grateful memory, undimmed through these fifty years, of that pleasant visit to Brookhill.

I count it among the chief joys of my life to claim the friendship of Mr. and Mrs. John Stewart and their devoted daughters.

Miss Mary married Capt. Thomas Pinckney, A.S.C., Miss Belle (Isobel) married my friend Joseph Bryan, of Laburnum, Miss Marion married my friend George W. Peterkin, now Bishop of West Virginia, the other four daughters — Misses Annie, Lucy, Norma and Hope remain unmarried.

Shortly after this W.H.F. Lee's Division marched down the Chickahominy River and took position on the extreme right of the Army, near Malvern Hill, observing the movement of Gen. Grant's Army. One Sunday morning — about the 12th of June — I rode with my brother-staff officer, Lieut. Frank S. Robertson, to the crest of Malvern Hill to spend the Sabbath resting and lounging in the shade of the trees, and watching the Yankee gun-boats lying off in the long reaches of the James River. All was quiet along the lines, and we enjoyed the view over the tree tops at the enemy's fleet. Soon one of their gunboats steamed up stream, the lookout having spied our horses against the sky-line, and in another moment we were saluted by the roar of a big shell and the boom of the heavy gun, almost simultaneous with the rush of the shell overhead. Jumping into our saddles we galloped rapidly from the spot and before we could count the distance, a second shell passed between our horses

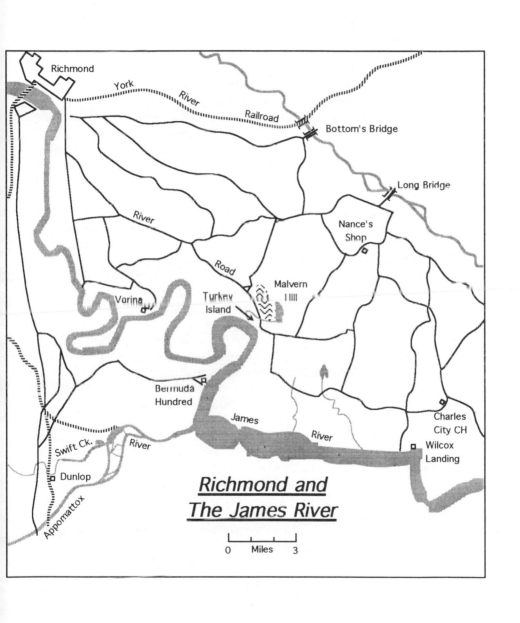

Richmond

York

River

Railroad

Bottom's Bridge

Long Bridge

River

Nance's
Shop

Road

Malvern

Varina

Turkey
Island

Bermuda
Hundred

James

Charles
City CH

River

Wilcox
Landing

Swift Ck.

River

Dunlop

Appomattox

*Richmond and
The James River*

0   Miles   3

and exploded about 50 yards ahead of us, tearing up a cartload of earth and sod. Veering off we hastened out of the line of fire, and with this the bombardment ceased. We made our way to camp rather disgruntled at having our Sunday spoilt, but congratulating ourselves that it was no worse. There we learned that a few days before, one of our pickets at or near Turkey Island, just below Malvern Hill, had been fired at by a Yankee gunboat, the shell striking him as he sat in his saddle — and cutting his body in two.

For a day or two after this there was no movement worthy of note, but on the 14th June orders were received at Division Headquarters and we moved with the North Carolina Brigade down the River Road, crossing Turkey Island Creek, having ascertained that Grant's Army had marched and were crossing the James River near Willcox's [sic] Landing. Gen. W.H.F. Lee gave me permission to move ahead of our column, and I rode rapidly to Willcox's [sic] farm without encountering or overtaking the enemy's rear-guard. With my field-glasses I watched the last of Grant's cavalry crossing the pontoon-bridge and viewed the encampment of the vast trains and quartermaster transportation stretching along the opposite shore. A forest of masts crowded the southern shore and armed vessels lay in the river. I could read the names of several large steamers and one or two ugly looking customers had up steam and were moving slowly up and down stream. It was not long before the head of our column came in sight and halted back on the River Road, its flank exposed to any fire that might come from the gun-boats in the river. Two guns of McGregor's Battery galloped across the wide, open plain a few hundred yards west of the Willcox [sic] house, and taking position close to the edge of the high bluff, which here overlooked the whole panorama, opened a brisk fire upon the shipping and the enemy generally. The guns were too close to the bluff and could not be depressed sufficiently to do much damage, and so McGregor turned them on the wagon camps on the opposite bank. The distance was very great and only a few shells burst among them, but instantly there was a great commotion, the mules breaking away and scampering off up the slopes of the River bank, while their drivers and the men from the tents looked like an army of ants stampeded out of their little hills. Only a few rounds had been fired when a long, low-lying, dun-colored gun-boat came slowly up stream, and before she arrived fairly opposite to the position of our battery, Capt. McGregor gave his order to "limber up" and we retired — just in time to escape destruction. As we were driving back across the open plain, a heavy shell passed over the battery, in exact line, and burst with tremendous force, only a short distance ahead of us in front of the leading gun. Before we got out of the field another shell passed over us and struck in our column as it stood in the main road, with its exposed flank, killing two men and horses. The column was speedily moved, and night coming on we marched back to our old position near Malvern Hill.

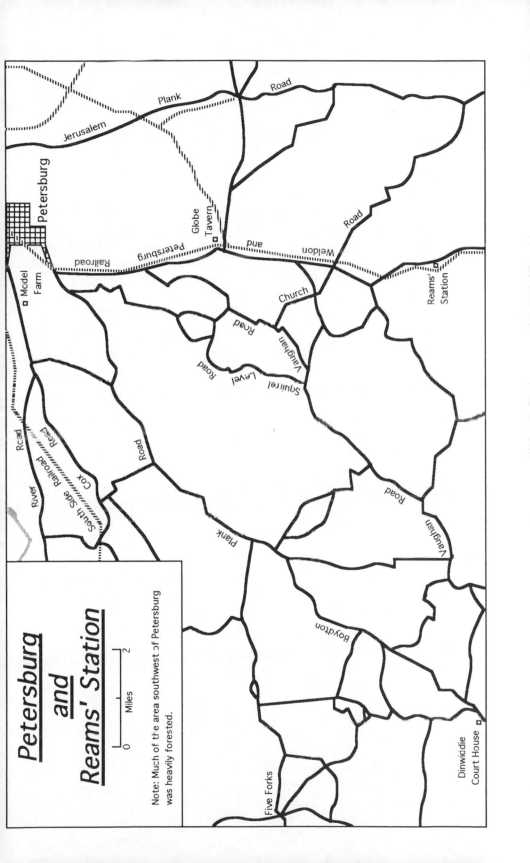

Petersburg
and
Reams' Station

Miles
0 — 2

Note: Much of the area southwest of Petersburg was heavily forested.

Petersburg

Model Farm

Jerusalem Plank Road

Globe Tavern

Petersburg Railroad

Petersburg and Weldon Railroad

Church Road

Reams' Station

River

Cox Road

South Side Railroad

Road

Squirrel Level Road

Vaughan Road

Plank Road

Vaughan Road

Boydton

Five Forks

Dinwiddie Court House

On the 16th our Division crossed the James and marched for Petersburg. Gen. Lee permitted Lieut. Frank Robertson and myself to ride into Richmond — where we treated ourselves to a good, substantial dinner, at a cost in Confederate money too extravagant for mention. After which we mounted our weary horses and marched to Petersburg, joining our Headquarters. on Swift Creek, near Dunlop's house.

Next day the Division moved through Petersburg and camped beyond the "Model Farm" where we remained for two or three days.

Chambliss' Brigade — 9th, 10th, and 13th Virginia Cavalry had been left behind and was still on the north side of the James, near Nance's Shop, where it rendered gallant and effective service in the severe engagements with Sheridan's command, aiding Generals Hampton and Fitz Lee on their return from the Trevillian's [sic] Campaign, and driving off all the Federal cavalry in that vicinity.

At Petersburg the Brigade of Cavalry commanded by General James Dearing was added to Genl. W.H.F. Lee's Division — and with it came Captain [Edward] Graham's Battery of Horse Artillery — a very gallant and well drilled company of Petersburg, whose service in all our subsequent campaigns were [sic] most valuable and distinguished.

General Dearing was a fine soldier. Brave, energetic and daring, his course at West Point had been interrupted by the war, and he entered the Confederate Army serving brilliantly in the Artillery as Major of Battalion. Promoted to Brigadier he was given a brigade consisting of the 4th North Carolina, Col. D.D. [Colonel Dennis Dozier] Ferebee, the 16th Battalion North Carolina Cavalry, Lt. Col. [Lieutenant Colonel Thomas] Boyd Edelin, and a few companies of Georgia Cavalry, which I think were known as the 7th Regulars — Confederate States Cavalry.

It was too small a command for such an officer as Gen. Dearing, but he added to his already fine reputation by skillful handling and hard fighting, and in the winter of 1865 he was promoted to the command of Rosser's old Brigade, then in the Valley of Virginia. On the retreat from Petersburg to Appomattox, General Dearing was killed in the fight near High Bridge, in personal combat with the Federal General Rice whom he slew as he received his own mortal wound.[61]

As we lay in our bivouac on the hard and dusty earth at the Model Farm our night's rest was disturbed by the incessant firing between the Infantry of both Armies in front of Petersburg. But on the ____ [exact date unknown] day of June 1864 orders came to break camp and move to Reams' Station, a point 10 miles south of Petersburg on the Weldon Railroad. Marching a half mile ahead of the column, with a small advance-guard, we had gotten nearly in sight of Reams' Station when I met one of our pickets retreating towards us, who informed me that his post had been taken by a small body of the enemy's cavalry who had established their picket at the forks of the road a short distance ahead.

Riding ahead with our advance-guard, I was surprised to see the enemy's picket-guard leave their post and take the road leading westward towards Dinwiddie Court House, instead of going eastward towards Reams'. Reporting this to Gen. W.H.F. Lee, he immediately ordered our column to follow the road to Dinwiddie Court House and we pushed on rapidly towards that place passing through it about sunset and moving on to Five Forks, where we encountered a strong rear guard of Wilson & [Brigadier General August Valentine] Kautz — the commencement of that remarkable Raid conducted by those two Federal Cavalrymen upon the Southside Railroad with about 5000 cavalry and three batteries of Horse Artillery, which ended in their complete discomfiture a week later at their point of departure — Reams' Station.[62]

The history of this Raid has never been fairly written, nor has Genl. W.H.F. Lee and the two brigades of his Division with him on his long pursuit of Wilson & Kautz ever received proper credit for their gallant service and heroic conduct on this trying expedition

— POSTLUDE —

The memoir abruptly ends here. Whether Garnett added to it is unknown. He evidently planned to do so (his remark that he would have much to say about his service with Brig. Gen. William P. Roberts' brigade indicates this), but nothing has been discovered. Garnett's last entry was dated May 5, 1913 almost two years before his death. As with the missing first part of the sketches the story of Garnett's service with the cavalry as it rode to Appomattox will remain an intriguing mystery.

Part III

Introduction

WHEN MAJOR GENERAL J.E.B. Stuart died on May 12, 1864 Theodore S. Garnett, his aide-de-camp, undoubtedly believed his duty to his gallant chief was ended. In the course of time, however, Garnett was to discover that he had one more obligation to fulfill. The moment to render that final service came on May 30, 1907 before a crowd of thousands present to witness the unveiling of an equestrian statue sculpted in the dashing image of Stuart, "the eyes" of Robert E. Lee's Army of Northern Virginia.

The course of events that brought Garnett to the podium that day began in May 1875 when the Richmond City Council passed a resolution calling for the erection of an equestrian statue of Stuart as soon as the city had means to accomplish it. There the matter rested until October 3, 1891, the date of the founding of the Veteran Cavalry Association of the Army of Northern Virginia. The original goal of the association was to place a suitable monument on Stuart's grave in Hollywood Cemetery. Within a short time that goal was refashioned to one of constructing an equestrian statue at a fitting location in the city.

At its founding the officers of the association were Gen. Fitzhugh Lee, president, Capt. Charles A. Taylor, secretary, and Mr. E.A. Catlin, treasurer. Lt. W. Ben Palmer became treasurer upon the death of Captain Taylor. The names of the individuals who served as vice-president read like a veritable Who's Who of the cavalry: Generals Wade Hampton, Lunsford L. Lomax, Matthew C. Butler, William P. Roberts, William H.F. Payne, Col. Thomas T. Munford, and Maj. Henry B. McClellan. The executive committee which assisted the officers of the association in their work consisted of many well-known ex-Confederates including Major Andrew R. Venable, Captain Theodore S. Garnett, and Private James Vass, all of whom had served among Stuart's staff or headquarters personnel.

The association began its work, and through donations, fund raisers, and collections the money necessary for the construction of the monument slowly accumulated. Eventually, assured of a sufficiency of funds, designs for the statue were accepted and the winner was Mr. Fred Moynihan of Brooklyn, New York. Moynihan brought distinguished credentials to the project, having assisted

Edward V. Valentine on the statue of Thomas Jefferson which graced the Jefferson Hotel. He had also worked on statues of "Stonewall" Jackson and William C. Wickham.

The design submitted by Moynihan, with small changes suggested by the Committee on Statue, consisting of General Fitzhugh Lee, Major Andrew R. Venable, Captain Theodore S. Garnett, and Captain M. J. Dimmock, was approved on May 10, 1904. Late that same month Mrs. J.E.B. Stuart journeyed from Norfolk to inspect the models. Her choice was in agreement with the committee's. Though the selection of Moynihan's design met with some opposition due to its similarity to sculptor Henry Foley's statue of British General Sir James Outram which stands in Calcutta, India, the work began on constructing the full size model from which the bronze statue would be cast.

Plans for the statue's unveiling were made to coincide with the Confederate Veterans reunion which was to take place between May 30 and June 3, 1907. In addition to Garnett several other members of the staff were present to participate in the ceremony. Former lieutenant and aide-de-camp Walter Q. Hullihen, then an Episcopal minister in Staunton, Virginia, rendered the prayer and Andrew R. Venable, one of Stuart's adjutant generals, introduced Garnett as the main speaker. Other members of the staff present were Chiswell Dabney, lieutenant and aide under Stuart, and Frank S. Robertson, lieutenant and assistant engineer officer.

The choice of Garnett as the one to deliver the dedication address was most fortunate. He had served with Stuart as part of the headquarters personnel (a clerk in the adjutant general's department) and as a staff officer. His period of service extended for almost a year from May 15, 1863 until Stuart's death. He was one of only two men to have served first as a member of the headquarters company and then as a officer of the staff (Lieutenant William "Henry" Hagan was the other), so he was able to view Stuart from two different vantage points.

As far as is known there is no copy of the speech in Garnett's handwriting. The only copies extant are from a printing of the speech by the Neale Publishing Company which first published it in December 1907 as "a correct outline of his career and a faithful tribute to the great commander of Lee's cavalry." The appendix which appeared only in the printed version is included here. Garnett wished to add his mite to the defense of his beloved commander who was being criticized for his role in the Gettysburg Campaign.

Of interest is the observation of Chiswell Dabney who sat three rows behind Garnett as he stood and delivered his address. Dabney observed that he could not hear a word of what Garnett was saying due to the noise of the crowd which he estimated at 50,000. Just how much anyone heard that day is unknown, but fortunately Garnett consented to have the speech published. Along with Henry B. McClellan's short biography of Stuart in his book *I Rode*

With Jeb Stuart, Garnett's sketch of Stuart's life remained one of the primary sources on the cavalry's commander until John W. Thomason's full biography, *Jeb Stuart*, appeared (first copyrighted in 1929). Many others have since written books and articles on Stuart's life and his role in the war, but Garnett was there, rode at Stuart's side, and was with him to and from Yellow Tavern. His eulogy to his commander and friend is still worth the reading.

MAJOR GENERAL THEODORE S. GARNETT, UNITED CONFEDERATE VETERANS
Courtesy of Mrs. Maria Hood

MAJOR GENERAL THEODORE S. GARNETT, UNITED CONFEDERATE VETERANS
(Others unidentified) *Courtesy of Mrs. Marla Hood*

Address Delivered At The Unveiling Of The Equestrian Statue Of General J.E.B. Stuart At Richmond, Virginia, May 30, 1907,

By Theodore S. Garnett, His A.D.C.

COMRADES OF THE Veteran Cavalry Association of the Army of Northern Virginia, United Confederate Veterans, Fellow Citizens of Richmond, Ladies and Gentlemen:

In response to a call as inspiring as the bugles of Stuart on the field of battle, I am here to attempt the impossible task which has been assigned me by my old comrades.

Forty-three years, to this same flowery month of May, have passed away since

> The cannon of his country pealed Stuart's funeral knell,

and that same period has elapsed since the city of Richmond registered its high resolve to place a monument here to his undying name.

To the honor of this city, and in proof of her gratitude for his sacrifice of life in her behalf, the city of Richmond, coming to the aid of the Veteran Cavalry Association of the Army of Northern Virginia, sees to-day the realization of hopes so long cherished by his faithful followers.

On the 14th day of May, 1864, at a meeting of the City Council of Richmond, General Randolph, after announcing to the Council the death of General Stuart, submitted the following resolution:

> *Whereas,* The people of Richmond, in common with their fellow-citizens of the Confederate States, have to deplore in the death of Major General J.E.B. Stuart, not only the loss of one of the first military characters of the age, but also of a citizen whose eminent patriotism and pure life gave the best guarantee that his great military capacity would never be otherwise employed than in the cause of freedom and for the welfare of his country; and

Whereas, They not only recognize this their great misfortune, in common with the rest of their countrymen, but bearing in mind that he yielded up his heroic spirit in the immediate defense of their city, and the successful effort to purchase their safety by the sacrifice of his own life, they are profoundly moved with sentiments of gratitude for his great services and of benevolent feeling for his glorious memory, and are desirous to express and to record their sense of peculiar obligation in a permanent and emphatic manner; therefore be it

Resolved, That the Council of the city of Richmond, in behalf of the citizens thereof, tender to the family of General Stuart the deepest and most heartfelt condolence, and earnestly request that the remains of their great benefactor may be permitted to rest under the eye and guardianship of the people of Richmond, and that they may be allowed to commemorate by a suitable monument their gratitude and his services.

A further resolution was adopted appointing a committee of three, Messrs. Randolph, Denton, and Hill,

To report a design for a suitable monument and inscription at some future meeting of the body.

War, with its relentless fury, swept onward over every foot of Virginia soil. The enemy, in ever-increasing hosts, encompassed you about and sat down over against this devoted city — the Capital of the Confederacy — and within a twelve-month the bitter fate that had been averted from you by Stuart and his troopers, swiftly and suddenly descended upon you.

The days of our years of destruction and reconstruction have been many and full of sorrow, but to-day we behold a resurrection and ascension as marvelous as it is glorious. Your city is not only rebuilt, but it has expanded beyond imagination. Where we now stand was then the open country. The triumphant march of progress has opened up this magnificent Monument Avenue, crowned as it is by the imposing statue of General Lee and the memorial to President Jefferson Davis. Into this goodly company we come now to place the heroic statue of a man who,

Take him for all in all
We ne'er shall look upon his like again.

JAMES EWELL BROWN STUART was born in Patrick County, Virginia, on the 6th day of February, 1833.

He was the youngest son of Archibald Stuart and Elizabeth, his wife; and whether or not our democratic simplicity attaches any significance to his alleged descent from the royal line of Scotland's kings, we who knew this true son of Virginia make bold to declare that no prince of the blood ever did more honor to an illustrious ancestry. Strong in mind and body, educated in the three cardinal virtues of Virginia youth, he grew up to manhood a splendid specimen of the hardy young mountaineer, and fresh from the meadows and pinnacles of the Dan, he took his place among the boys at West Point, and there learned the science that

Teacheth the hands to war and the fingers to fight.

Noted in this famous school as the most daring and skillful horseman among all his fellows, he sought and obtained active duty as a lieutenant in the Second U.S. Cavalry, then engaged in an arduous expedition against the Indians of the Southwest.

In close encounter with this subtle enemy he received a severe wound — the only injury he ever suffered until his fatal wounding in his last battle. Soon recovering, he was sent to the plains of Kansas, where his command vainly strove to keep the peace between the warring factions of Northern and Southern settlers — the first mutterings of the storm which soon broke upon our country in the whirlwind of civil war.

In October, 1859, as aide-de-camp to Colonel Robert E. Lee at Harper's Ferry, he bore the summons to John Brown to surrender himself and his fanatic followers to the authority of the United States and to Virginia, whose peace and dignity they had criminally violated. With grim humor old Ossawattomie Brown told the young man how easily he could have taken his life, as he felt tempted to do, when Lieutenant Stuart approached the engine-house door and demanded his surrender.

Such, in brief, was his preparation for the great career on which he entered in 1861.

To his old comrades here, and to most of those who were in other arms of the service, it is a thrice-told tale to recount his mighty deeds, his prowess in battle, his sleepless vigilance, his unerring judgment in strategy and attack, his faith in our cause, and his devotion to duty. But it is right, on this historic occasion, when his memory rises for the coronation of this hour, to take brief note of the achievements of this great commander of the cavalry of the Army of Northern Virginia.

Identified with that army from its first skirmish to the day of his death, he knew no other duty nor any loftier ambition than to serve

The cause of freedom and the welfare of his country.

With all his soul he loved his country. No patriot in all the tide of time ever worshiped at the pure shrine of Liberty with nobler devotion than he. As we were bringing him mortally wounded off the field at Yellow Tavern, he exclaimed with intense feeling to some who were retreating by him: "Go back, my men, go back! and do your duty as I have done mine, and our country will be free."

Bear with me, then, while I hasten through the thrilling record of his wonderful and brilliant career.

From the day when, with a small force, he captured an entire company of the enemy's infantry near the Potomac, to the hour of that fatal charge in which he received his death-wound, there was not a moment of his life which lacked the inspiration of his high ambition or the tireless energy of his zealous soul.

Pressing forward his handful of cavalry, through byways and difficult paths, he passed from rear to front of Johnston's column on the march from the Valley to first Manassas, eager to be in at the death of McDowell's army. There, at the crucial moment, he led a mounted charge into the midst of the Federal infantry, breaking their lines and precipitating the disorder which soon became a panic and a rout more complete than any ever afterward seen on the field of battle. Of this movement General Early, in his official report, says:

> Stuart did as much toward saving the battle of First Manassas as any subordinate who participated in it.

From Manassas to the Peninsula, now as a brigade commander, he served General Johnston with such indefatigable skill as to merit that great General's heartiest acknowledgment, and wrung from him, afterward, when separated, the deep lament: "How can I eat or sleep in any peace without you on the outpost!"

The crossing of sabers at Williamsburg was the beginning of the long list of cavalry battles in which Stuart's genius for war shone so conspicuously bright, and in which he taught his troopers the lessons from which the cavalry of Europe now seek their inspiration and education.

The engagements along the Chickahominy made manifest the superiority of Stuart's cavalry over McClellan's, and here, for the first time, a feat then unparalleled in war was accomplished, which it is doubtful whether any other man than Stuart would have dared to attempt. This first raid around McClellan's army, not only made him famous as a cavalry leader, but blazed the way for that grand strategy of General Lee which brought Jackson from the Valley and overwhelmed McClellan in the Seven Days' battles.

The march of General Stuart in June, 1862, with 1200 men and two guns under Lieutenant Breathed of the Stuart Horse Artillery, making the entire circuit of McClellan's army, with the loss of one officer, the gallant Captain William Latane, of the Essex Troop, was an achievement not only unique in war, but the information thus obtained was the moving cause of the defeat of McClellan's entire campaign.

Speedily assembling his command in July of that year, when his well-won commission as major-general was conferred upon him, he hastened to the assistance of Jackson in the campaign against Pope, and again in the rear of the enemy he captured Manassas and played havoc with the supplies and communications of Pope's army.

An English military critic has recently recorded this opinion:

> Without the help which Stuart was able to give, the flank march around Pope's army by Jackson's corps and the concentration of the two Confederate wings on the battlefield of Manassas, would not have been possible — "Crisis of the Confederacy," p. 392.

Then crossing the Potomac, Stuart occupied the rich pastures of Maryland and protected the cantonments of General Lee as his army rested at Frederick, recuperating its strength for the fierce encounter at Sharpsburg. Here he took position on the left of Jackson's corps and held off the masses which threatened to envelop and destroy our exposed left wing, thus rendering possible the bloody repulse inflicted upon McClellan's preponderant forces.

Returning to Virginia, he conceived and executed a second expedition around McClellan's host, via Chambersburg and the enemy's rear, recrossing the Potomac into Virginia after inflicting great losses, capturing prisoners, horses, and transportation, and putting to flight all McClellan's dreams of conquest. So great, indeed, was the effect of this movement that President Lincoln indulged his sarcastic humor at the expense of McClellan, laughing to scorn the alleged brokendown condition of his cavalry, and placing on record the President's own testimony to the fact that Stuart's cavalry had "outmarched and outfought" its opponents, and was still ready for battle. This fact, so plain to Mr. Lincoln and Mr. Stanton, after the Chambersburg raid, caused the loss of McClellan's official head, and Burnside supplanted him.

The long march to Fredericksburg soon followed, and great credit must be awarded to Stuart for the masterly handling of his small forces in protecting the exposed flank of our army as it marched eastward to interpose between Richmond and the heavy advancing columns of Burnside. Day after day our cavalry met the enemy's in severe and incessant combat, while the army pursued the even tenor of its way, undisturbed by the distant thunder of our guns and the shock of charging squadrons.

So was it ever with us, my comrades, and our brethren of the infantry and artillery. While the Army of Northern Virginia slept in peace, Stuart on the outpost made their rest secure. If the men composing Stuart's Cavalry Corps were not worthy of the best troops of any army, then it is vain to seek for soldiers in any part of this world.

Brother Cavalrymen! I salute you, survivors of a body of horsemen worthy of King Arthur, Richard Coeur de Leon, Godfrey de Bouillon, Prince Rupert and his Cavaliers, Cromwell and his troopers, or the greatest of all cavalrymen, Robert E. Lee!

FREDERICKSBURG

What a splendid panorama was unfolded to your steady gaze as the fog lifted above the snowy canopy of that rolling plain, disclosing in vast array the long blue lines of battle. On the right near Hamilton's crossing, Stuart attacked the enemy, and with impetuous dash he led his horse artillery, under the gallant Pelham, into the jaws of death, hammered the flank of Meade's grand division, and with two guns, far to the front, opposed a multitude of batteries, breaking their lines and aiding most materially the victory won by Jackson and his indomitable veterans.

CHANCELLORSVILLE

Chancellorsville followed with the first breath of spring, and in its wonderful story is found the climax of Stuart's glorious career.

History and Art are fond of portraying the last meeting of Lee and Jackson. To those immortal names the great heart of the South instinctively adds, by common and universal consent, the name of Stuart as worthy to ride with them down the ages. In that last meeting the hand of Stuart clasped the hand of Jackson in a long farewell as Stuart moved in front to clear the way for the last great triumph and tragedy of Jackson's life. And when Lee's "right arm" was stricken helpless by that fearful accident, and Jackson lay bleeding on the fatal field, who of all that host could dare to grasp and wield the fallen chieftain's sword? Night had closed in upon the halting lines, and confusion worse confounded threatened to turn back the tide of victory. With the wounding of General A.P. Hill, and the noble self-denial of General Rodes, the command of Jackson's corps devolved upon General Stuart — the most trying responsibility that was ever forced upon any officer in any battle of the war.

"Send for General Stuart," said Jackson, and with this last order ever uttered by him on the field of his great glory, he added the noble sentence inscribed upon this monument:

Tell General Stuart to act upon his own judgment and do what he thinks best — I have implicit confidence in him.

With that message ringing in his ears, and inspired with superhuman energy, the young cavalryman spent the dark hours of that eventful night in ceaseless activity, restoring order out of chaos; and when the day dawned every man was in his place, the lines well drawn, and with a spirit as indomitable as Jackson's own, he hurled his troops in fresh onset upon the bristling ranks of the astonished foe. Crowning Hazel Grove with massed artillery, he swept away Hooker's last refuge, joined his right wing to the advancing troops under the eye of General Lee, and burst over the plateau of Chancellorsville with shouts of victory louder than the roar of battle.

You, his old troopers, who knew and loved him so well, need no other reason for your faith and pride in him than the fact that the names of Lee, Jackson, and Stuart are indissolubly linked together in the proud record which history has inscribed for him in the temple of fame.

A distinguished officer of the artillery of Longstreet's corps (General Alexander) has placed on record this tribute to Stuart, as true as it is generous, when he wrote:

> Altogether, I do not think there was a more brilliant thing done in the war than Stuart's extricating that command from the extremely critical position in which he found it, as promptly and boldly as he did. We knew that Hooker had at least 80,000 infantry at hand.... The hard marching and the night fighting had thinned our ranks to less than 20,000. But Stuart never seemed to hesitate or doubt for one moment.... He decided to attack at daybreak, and, unlike many planned attacks that I have seen, this one came off promptly on time, and it never stopped to draw its breath until it had crashed through everything, and our forces stood united around Chancellor's burning house.

And General Alexander adds:

> I always thought it an injustice to Stuart and a loss to the army that he was not from that moment continued in command of Jackson's corps. He had won the right to it. I believe he had all of Jackson's genius and dash and originality . . . . Stuart possessed the rare quality of being always equal to himself at his very best.

FLEETWOOD OR BRANDY STATION

I have said that Chancellorsville was the climax of Stuart's glory. It convinced the army of Stuart's power to handle large bodies of infantry and artillery in action, under desperate circumstances and against desperate odds.

We come now to the battle of Fleetwood, as he called it, but better known by his men as Brandy Station, June 9, 1863, in which we see him as the victor in the greatest cavalry battle of the nineteenth century.

General Pleasanton's twenty-four regiments of cavalry were supported by ten regiments of Federal infantry, while only fifteen regiments of Stuart's command were actually engaged in the battle, unsupported by any infantry whatever. Pleasanton's plan of battle was admirable. Under the gallant Gregg one division was thrown directly in rear of our line at Fleetwood Hill, while Buford with two divisions of his cavalry and one brigade of infantry assaulted our whole front at St. James' Church. By all the laws of war and chances of battle, Stuart should have been crushed and utterly destroyed. But by a rapid change of front to rear Stuart hastened to Fleetwood with regiment after regiment of Jones's and Hampton's brigades, and by a succession of most gallant and desperate charges wrested victory from the jaws of defeat and drove Gregg and Kilpatrick from the vantage ground of Fleetwood Hill.

No more brilliant spectacle was ever witnessed than the brave Hampton leading on his gallant Carolinians, as with flashing sabers they plunged into the masses of Gregg's troopers and scattered them far and wide. Nor will the saber ever play a more glorious part in battle than did that day the shining blades of the Virginians under Harman, Elijah White, Lindsay Lomax, and Flournoy, and of the North Carolinians under Lawrence Baker, the South Carolinians under Black, the Georgians under Young, and the Mississippians under Waring. I mention these glorious names not because they excelled in valor the steady work of W.H.F. Lee's brigade and the Seventh Virginia Cavalry and others, who held back the two divisions of Buford, but because it was vouchsafed to them to show the world that the saber is, after all, the weapon for grand cavalry battle.

For partisan warfare, or Indian and cowboy skirmishes, let the pistol and carbine hold undisputed sway; but for the fields on which thousands of cavalry strive for mastery in the shock of great battle, may the sabers of Stuart, of Forrest, and of Hampton ever lead the charging squadrons to victory or death.

GETTYSBURG

The campaign of Gettysburg commenced with a series of cavalry fights in Loudoun and Fauquier. For five days Stuart was constantly engaged with Pleasanton's whole corps, who, supported by the infantry, assumed the offensive and displayed an energy and audacity which would otherwise never have been exhibited. The resulting losses were severe, and when we commenced the long march to the enemy's rear, threatening Washington City, our men and horses were already worn and jaded.

The fact that it took Stuart one day longer than he expected to fight his way to Carlisle, Pennsylvania, arriving on the field of Gettysburg on the second day of the battle, has been used to account for the failure of the Army of Northern Virginia to keep up its unbroken score of victories.

To say that the battle would have been won if Stuart had arrived a day earlier is a tribute to him greater than his most ardent admirers could claim.

General Lee believed that if Stonewall Jackson had been there the victory would have been assured. But Stuart was as blameless for his march to Carlisle as Jackson was for his absence in another and better world. The charge that Stuart's march from the Potomac to the Susquehanna was not warranted by his orders or by the best military judgment at that time, has been completely refuted by the masterly pens of Colonel John S. Mosby and Major H. B. McClellan, based on the official records.

General Lee's letters to Stuart on the 22nd and 23rd of June, 1863, [see Appendix] establish the fact that General Lee authorized Stuart to use his discretion as to crossing the Potomac by way of the enemy's rear, and General Longstreet, who communicated to him those instructions, distinctly advised General Stuart to choose that route. Two brigades of cavalry (Robertson and Jones) were left on the Blue Ridge to watch Hooker's army on the Potomac and keep General Lee advised of Hooker's movements, while Stuart with his other three brigades moved on through Maryland. A cavalry fight at Hanover took place on June 30th with Kilpatrick's division. It caused a wide detour, in the course of which we crossed the trail of Early's division. General Early heard our guns at Hanover and rightly conjectured that they were Stuart's Horse Artillery. Strangely and unhappily he failed to communicate with Stuart or leave any intimation that he was on the march for Cashtown.

Napoleon's guns at Waterloo were heard by Grouchy on the road to Wavre, and if he had crossed over to the Emperor's assistance the story of Waterloo would have been differently told. But no sound of Ewell's battle on the 1st of July at Gettysburg reached Stuart's ears as he pressed on to Carlisle, where he expected to find the right wing of General Lee's army. Therefore it happened that the cavalry attacked Carlisle, and there, near midnight, by the glare of the burning Barracks, Stuart read the dispatch announcing the victory of Ewell and Hill over the Federal forces. Instantly the attack on Carlisle was abandoned, and by a hard night march we pressed south to Gettysburg, arriving just as Ewell was beginning his assault upon Culp's Hill on the evening of the second day's battle.

It is needless to tell you of the severe cavalry fight on July 3rd between Stuart and Gregg on our extreme left — a position which we held as the battle closed, and which was of critical value if the charge of Pickett and Pettigrew had resulted as General Lee expected.

To those who know General Stuart's character as we knew it, the bare suggestion that he was capable of disobeying any order of General Lee, either in letter or in spirit, is not only incredible, but absolutely untrue. General Lee himself, in his official report, makes not the slightest intimation of such a monstrous impossibility.

Colonel Mosby, in righteous indignation, has exclaimed:

How could Stuart join Ewell on the Susquehanna, guard the gaps of the Blue Ridge in Virginia, watch and impede Hooker's crossing of the Potomac, and then place himself on the right of our column as it advanced into Pennsylvania, unless he was inspired with ubiquity? Even Hercules could not perform all of his twelve labors at the same time.

The last word has not yet been said about Gettysburg. It will be discussed long after Waterloo has been forgotten, but history will not permit the fame of Stuart to be tarnished by the false claim that he disobeyed any order ever received by him from General Lee.

His conduct in reaching the battlefield as soon as he did is as praiseworthy as his invaluable service on the retreat to the Potomac. Of this service the author of the "Crisis of the Confederacy," a trained military critic, says:

That Lee brought his forces out of this dilemma, not only without serious loss but with an air of reluctantly relinquishing the theatre, was due to the skill of his dispositions and to the admirable coordination of the movements of his lieutenants; but the march was only possible, thanks to the bold and skillful handling of the cavalry by Stuart, who excelled himself in these dark days of misfortune.

And the same excellent authority says:

Stuart's indefatigable horsemen could be counted on to render valuable help in delaying the enemy's advance and guarding the left, which was the exposed flank, if the enemy should venture to attack. All day on July 8th, while the cavalry was fighting, the Confederate army rested after the feat of marching which had brought it from Gettysburg to the Potomac.

Bear in mind that in this retreat Stuart was suffering from the loss of many of his best officers killed, and among the severely wounded was the gallant Hampton, whose services for many days were lost to the cavalry.

Time does not permit, nor will your patience allow, even a brief outline of Stuart's further service in the last year of his life. Twice more on the field of Brandy Station he encountered the enemy's cavalry, and each time drove him back across the Rappahannock. And in the Bristoe campaign he scattered the command and well-nigh ruined the reputation of General Kilpatrick at the "Buckland races." The Mine Run campaign with its intense cold and suffering soon followed, and after Meade's retreat from Mine Run with an army more than double that of General Lee, we settled down in winter quarters at Orange, awaiting the final struggle in northern Virginia.

The official records give no sign of the tremendous effort put forth by Stuart to overcome the disparity of force then existing and daily increasing between Stuart and Sheridan. With less than half his cavalry mounted, General Stuart moved against the twelve thousand cavalry of Sheridan, and in the Wilderness, at Todd's Tavern, and Spottsylvania Court House he neutralized the vast body of cavalry attending Grant's army.

On Monday, May 9, 1864, Sheridan with 10,000 well-mounted and equipped cavalry and several batteries of artillery, flanking our extreme right at Spottsylvania Court House, marched rapidly south to capture and destroy the city of Richmond. Promptly Stuart moved with two brigades of Fitz Lee's division, Wickham and Lomax, leaving orders for Gordon with his North Carolina brigade to follow fast. A severe fight with Sheridan's rearguard took place that evening, and next day we pressed the rapidly moving enemy until Stuart succeeded in placing his two brigades in close contact with Sheridan's immense force, and boldly gave him battle at Yellow Tavern.

For several hours Sheridan's whole column was checked. Gordon's brigade had attacked his rear many miles distant on the Mountain road, and so was separated from Stuart in the hour of his greatest need. Toward evening, after much fighting, with nearly our whole force dismounted, Sheridan, confident in the overwhelming numbers of his mounted troops, threw his heavy regiments, squadron after squadron, in a mounted charge upon our exposed left flank and broke through our artillery with resistless force.

Capturing three of our guns, the head of the enemy's column became engaged with our dismounted men and were suddenly checked in their advance. They had passed by General Stuart, who had emptied his pistol at them and was sitting quietly on his horse as they hastened back by him on their return. Man after man fired upon him without hitting him, until nearly the last one of them dashed past, and putting his pistol close up to his side fired the fatal bullet and hastened away. The General was taken from his horse by Captain Gus Dorsey, of Maryland, of Company K, First Virginia Cavalry, Stuart's old regiment, and then reviving a little from the shock, he was placed on the horse of Private Fred L. Pitts of that company, and led to an ambulance in the rear of the line. In this connection the names of Corporal Robert Bruce and Private Charles Wheatley are mentioned by Captain Dorsey as having rendered gallant service in removing the General to the ambulance, thus saving him from capture by the enemy. Thus safely brought off the field by the assistance of some of his staff, among them Major A. R. Venable, his gallant and devoted Inspector-General, he reached Richmond by way of Mechanicsville about eleven o'clock that night. He died here on the evening of May 12, 1864. Death never claimed a nobler victim.

Thus fell the matchless leader of the Veteran Cavalry of the Army of Northern Virginia.

We come not now to mourn his loss. That has been one long lamentation throughout the years which have crowded out the recollection of his brave deeds. But we, his brothers-in-arms, partakers of his glory, assemble here in loving fellowship to commemorate his services in this enduring and fitting monument.

The sculptor, Moynihan, has shared with us the inspiration of Stuart's career, and has fashioned both horse and rider with the spirit that animated his great soul. Idealized, it may be, to a degree that speaks eloquently of the superb horseman, the alert, active, dashing leader of brave men, it is at the same time a likeness of the man just as he was when General Sedgwick, his old commander, in rude appraisement, exclaimed: "Stuart is the best cavalry officer ever foaled in North America!"

The military student of Great Britain and the Continent is never weary of studying the campaigns of Stuart. One of them has recently written:

> To Stuart belongs the credit of having brought to perfection a use of the cavalry arm which had been foreshadowed by the dragoons of Marlborough's epoch, but which had not been seen during the intervening great wars of Europe, *nor has it ever yet been successfully imitated.*

In the bold combination of *fire* and *shock* at the right moment, Stuart's cavalry stands pre-eminent among the nations of the world. What loftier tribute can be paid to the heroes of our corps, living and dead, whose proudest boast, either in the triumphs of life or in the agonies of death, is Stuart's great name! Drilled and disciplined by him, they learned the severe lessons of outpost duty, sleepless vigilance, patient endurance and skill in battle, until they became the steady reliance of General Lee in all his campaigns — the eyes and ears of the Army of Northern Virginia.

Day after day the bravest and best were slain in battle. Innumerable skirmishes diminished our numbers as sorely as the losses of our infantry in many pitched battles, until our weary men with starving horses could scarce disguise the fact that we were fighting against hope.

The late Colonel Henderson, of the British Army, the brilliant author of "The Life of Stonewall Jackson," has left this tribute to the veteran cavalry of both armies:

> It may, however, be unhesitatingly admitted that no cavalry of the nineteenth century, except the American, could have achieved the same results...
> And it may be just as unhesitatingly declared that the horseman of the American war is the model of the efficient cavalryman.

THE STUART HORSE ARTILLERY.

Attached to the cavalry corps was one of the bravest and most efficient organizations that any army ever possessed. The Stuart Horse Artillery, from a single company commanded by the Gallant Pelham, grew into several battalions under Beckham, Breathed, Hart, McGregor, Chew, and Thompson, whose distinguished services are worthy of the most brilliant pages of our history. Would that time permitted me to render to the officers and men of those splendid horse-batteries the tribute they so well deserve!

The honor of firing the first gun at Fort Sumter is no longer in doubt. The proud distinction of firing the last gun at Appomattox is claimed by many, but the command that fired the most shot and shell, first, last and all the time, is perhaps, without doubt, the ever-glorious and gallant Stuart Horse Artillery.

Welcome, also, my comrades of Mosby's Battalion! In close affiliation with Stuart, nurtured and encouraged by him, valued and praised by him beyond measure, was the Forty-third Battalion of Virginia Cavalry, under the brave, skillful, and distinguished commander, Colonel John S. Mosby. Their heroic deeds form part of the glory achieved by the army, and we link their names with the cavalry corps in loving fellowship and everlasting honor.

And now, my Comrades, our task is done. This day, so long expected, has come at last to bless our vision and rejoice our hearts. Again Stuart rides with his great Commander who himself wrote the epitaph of his Chief of Cavalry. In official orders announcing his death to the army, May 20, 1864, General Lee said:

> Among the gallant soldiers who have fallen in this war General Stuart was second to none in valor, in zeal, and in unflinching devotion to his country. His achievements form a conspicuous part of the history of this army, with which his name and services will be forever associated. To military capacity of a high order and to the nobler virtues of the soldier he added the brighter graces of a pure life, guided and sustained by the Christian's faith and hope. The mysterious hand of an all-wise God has removed him from the scene of his usefulness and fame.

And he added these words, carved upon this monument and graven in our hearts:

> His grateful countrymen will mourn his loss and cherish his memory. To his comrades in arms he has left the proud recollection of his deeds and the inspiring influence of his example.

Once more Stuart rides with Lee, and again I see him, as on the plains of Brandy, the phantom horsemen pass him in review — their survivors, on the eve of life's last battle, exclaiming now as then, *"Te morituri salutamus !"*

Some of Stuart's pupils in the art of war have grown wiser, they think, than their master, and some have made bold to write themselves down as critics after the event. General Lee once wrote that even as poor a general as he himself was could see what might have been done after the battle was over. It has been truly said that the general who never made a mistake never fought a battle.

But now, waiving all controversy and comparison, Stuart stands upon the record inscribed upon this monument. The testimony of two witnesses is true: the witnesses are Stonewall Jackson and Robert E. Lee.

To the city of Richmond as its faithful guardian we commit this monument, in whose care and keeping it will henceforth stand, in token of a people's gratitude and in perpetual memory of his heroic name.

STUART

"I've called his name, a statue stern and vast,
It rests enthroned upon the mighty past,
Fit plinth for him whose image in the mind
Looms up as that of one by God designed.
Fit plinth, in sooth! the mighty past for him,
Whose simple name is Glory's synonym.
E 'en Fancy's self in her enchanted sleep
Can dream no future which may cease to keep
His name in guard, like sentinel, and cry
From Time's great bastions: 'It shall never
die !' "

— APPENDIX —

Correspondence Relating to Stuart's Role in the Gettysburg Campaign

HEADQUARTERS, June 22, 1863.

Major-General J.E.B. Stuart,
  Commanding Cavalry.
  General: — I have just received your note of 7:45 this morning to General Longstreet. I judge the efforts of the enemy yesterday were to arrest our progress and ascertain our whereabouts. Perhaps he is satisfied. Do you know where he is, and what he is doing? I fear he will steal a march on us, and get across the Potomac before we are aware. If you find he is moving northward and that two brigades can guard the Blue Ridge and take care of your rear, you can move with the other three into Maryland, and take position on General Ewell's right, place yourself in communication with him, guard his flank, keep him informed of the enemy's movements, and collect all the supplies you can for the use of the army. One column of General Ewell's army will probably move toward the Susquehanna by the Emmittsburg route; another by Chambersburg. . .
  I am very respectfully your obedient servant,

R.E. Lee,
General.

At 3:30 p.m. on the same day General Lee writes to General Ewell as follows:

I also directed General Stuart, should the enemy have so far retired from his front as to permit the departure of a portion of the cavalry, to march with three brigades across the Potomac, and place himself on your right and in communication with you, keep you advised of the movements of the enemy, and assist in collecting supplies for the army. I have not heard from him since. . . . .

Headquarters, Millwood,
June 22, 1863, 7 p.m.

Major-General J.E.B. Stuart,
  Commanding Cavalry.
  General: — General Lee has enclosed to me this letter for you to be forwarded to you, provided you can be spared from my front, and provided I think that you

can move across the Potomac without disclosing our plans. He speaks of you leaving by Hopewell Gap, and passing by the rear of the enemy. If you can get through by that route I think you will be less likely to indicate what our plans are, than if you should cross by passing to our rear. I forward the letter of instructions with these suggestions.

Please advise me of the condition of affairs before you leave, and order General Hampton — whom I suppose you will leave here in command — to report to me at Millwood, either by letter or in person, as may be most agreeable to him.

> Most respectfully,
> James Longstreet,
> Lieutenant General.

N.B. — I think that your passage of the Potomac by our rear at the present moment will, in a measure, disclose our plans. You had better not leave us, therefore, unless you can take the proposed route in rear of the enemy.

Having sent this letter to Stuart, General Longstreet writes as follows to General Lee:

HEADQUARTERS, June 22, 1863, 7:30 p.m.
General R. E. Lee, Commanding, etc.
    General: Yours of 4 o'clock this afternoon is received. I have forwarded your letter to General Stuart, with the suggestion that he pass by the enemy's rear if he thinks that he may get through. We have nothing from the enemy to-day.

> Most respectfully,
> James Longstreet,
> Lieutenant-General Commanding.

HEADQUARTERS, ARMY OF NORTHERN VIRGINIA,
June 23, 1863, 5 p.m.

Major-General J.E.B. Stuart,
    Commanding Cavalry.
    General: — Your notes of 9 and 10:30 a.m. to-day have just been received. As regards the purchase of tobacco for your men, supposing that Confederate money will not be taken, I am willing for your commissaries or quartermasters to purchase this tobacco, and let the men get it from them, but I can have nothing seized by the men.

If General Hooker's army remains inactive, you can leave two brigades to watch him, and withdraw with the three others; but should he not appear to be moving northward, I think you had better withdraw this side of the mountain tomorrow night, cross at Shepherdstown the next day, and move over to Fredericktown.

You will however be able to judge whether you can pass around their army without hindrance, doing them all the damage you can, and cross the river east of the mountains. In either case, after crossing the river, you must move on, and feel the right of Ewell's troops, collecting information, provisions, etc.

I am very respectfully and truly yours,

R.E. Lee,
General.

This correspondence shows that General Lee gave General Stuart full discretion as to where he should cross the Potomac River into Maryland — either east or west of the Blue Ridge Mountains. The eastern crossing necessarily involved his going "by the enemy's rear," thus passing between Hooker's army and Washington. It was impossible to pass between Hooker's position and Harper's Ferry. So implicit was Gen. Lee's confidence in Stuart that he finally tells him to determine this question for himself.

When General Stuart, after passing through the gap in the Bull Run Mountains, struck the rear of Hancock's corps and attacked it, he found that corps moving north toward Leesburg. The way to the Potomac was clearly open via Fairfax Court House, and he chose that route.

The only alternative then presented to Stuart's mind was to retrace his steps by a long march and follow Longstreet's corps, then moving northward through the Valley. This would have practically deprived the army of any aid from Stuart for several days, and left the enemy's cavalry free to attack General Lee at any point along his line of march.

The course adopted by General Stuart rendered Meade's cavalry of little use to him, two divisions of it having been sent off to look for Stuart. They found him at Hanover, Pa., on June 30, where a sharp encounter took place; but the march to Carlisle, as contemplated in his instructions from General Lee, was resumed and he reached that place on July 1, much sooner than he could have done by any other route.

Meantime, General Lee changed his mind and determined to concentrate his army near Cashtown; orders so to do were in process of execution when Heth's division advanced toward Gettysburg, and contrary to orders brought on the engagement of July 1. But for this action the whole army would have been assembled at Cashtown — infantry, artillery and cavalry — and the battle would never have been fought at Gettysburg. Nothing would ever have been written or said of General Lee's lack of information by reason of Stuart's absence on his long march, and it is more than probable that a great battle near Cashtown would have been a complete victory for General Lee.

T.S.G.

Notes to the Introduction to the Reminiscences

1 John Esten Cooke, "General Stuart in Camp and Field," *Annals of the War* (Philadelphia: The Times Publishing Company, 1879), p. 665.

2 The memoir contains seven dates which identify the periods when Garnett wrote — June 1, 1871, October 28, 1871, February 28, 1894, October 16, 1895, January 4, 1902, December 5, 1912 and May 5, 1913.

3 Von Borcke was recovering from the terrible wound he received at Upperville on June 19, 1863, as Stuart and the cavalry tried to keep Brig. Gen. Alfred Pleasonton from spying on Gen. Robert E. Lee's infantry during its movement north. Hairston had left the staff late in 1861, and Price and Hardeman Stuart were dead.

4 Philip H. Powers was no longer a staff officer, but he was attached to cavalry head-quarters as an assistant to Maj. Norman R. FitzHugh, the cavalry's quartermaster. A few of Powers's letters from that time survive. They reflect mostly personal and family concerns with only brief references to Stuart.

Notes to Continuation of War Sketches

1 Garnett's account of the cavalry's role in the Bristoe Station Campaign which began on October 9, 1863 is accurate. Major General Fitzhugh "Fitz" Lee crossed the Rapidan River on October 11, 1863 in pursuit of Brig. Gen. John Buford's command which had mounted a reconnaissance in force to discover Gen. Robert E. Lee's intentions. Buford had crossed the river at Germanna Ford and had moved toward Morton's Ford near where he encountered Col. Thomas Rosser's 5th Virginia Cavalry sent by Fitz Lee to oppose him. The action that followed eventually forced Buford to retreat across the river with Fitz Lee crossing at Morton's. The fighting around Brandy Station battlefield, which was the scene of numerous cavalry engagements throughout the war, described here by Garnett coincides with Stuart's report in general though the Union forces gave up their final position when threatened by a turning movement conducted by Fitz Lee under Stuart's orders. (U.S. War Department, *The War of the Rebellion: A Compilation of the Official Records of the Union and Confederate Armies*, Vol 29, Part 1, pp. 442-444; hereafter cited as *OR*, all references are to Series I.)

2 Capt. William Morrell McGregor led the 2nd Stuart Horse Artillery which had previously been commanded by Capt. Mathis W. Henry and had been formed by dividing Capt. John Pelham's original battery. McGregor, like Pelham, was from Alabama. Later in the war he rose to the rank of major and commanded a battalion of horse artillery. After the war he moved to Texas where he died on December 28, 1907. He is buried in Oak Hill Cemetery in Cameron, Texas.

3 The names of the men who so daringly slipped through the lines that night were Private Robert W. Goode of the 1st Virginia Cavalry, Private H. Hillery "Crocket" Eddins and Richard C. Baylor of the 12th Virginia Cavalry, and Sergeants Ashton Chichester and C.P. Shurley of Major William M. McGregor's Battery of the Stuart Horse Artillery.

4 This episode of Stuart being cut off from the army in the vicinity of Auburn can be verified through various accounts including the Official Records. Garnett's recollection of that tense night and subsequent escape corresponds with other personal accounts. (William W. Blackford, *War Years with Jeb Stuart*, pp. 238-240)

5 The debacle at Rappahannock bridge occurred on November 7, 1863 and coupled with a second attack at Kelly's Ford forced Gen. Robert E. Lee to retreat first to a line between Culpeper Court House and Brandy Station and finally across the Rapidan River.

Brig. Gen. Harry Hays, conducting a court of inquiry, was absent at the opening of the engagement, but returned in time to get captured when his lines were overrun. He later managed to escape when his horse bolted. In addition to Hay's Brigade Brig. Gen. Robert F. Hoke's Brigade, under the command of Col. Archibald C. Godwin, also suffered heavily in the engagement. Most of the casualties were prisoners. Garnett was not the only one in the army who felt that someone had blundered, but no blame was ever officially attached to anyone.

6   Known as the "Buckland Races," the action took place on October 19, 1863 and remains one of the most famous in the annals of the cavalry of the Army of Northern Virginia. The plan of operation was actually suggested to Stuart by Fitz Lee who felt he could better support his chief by attacking the enemy's rear as Stuart's retreated before them. A rousing chase of about three miles ensued resulting in the capture of 250 prisoners, a number of wagons (including Brigadier General George A. Custer's headquarters baggage) and numerous horses.

7   The individual Garnett referred to as "old Hagan" was Lt. William "Henry" Hagan, Stuart's Chief of Couriers and sometime commander of the General's escort. The "old" reflected Hagan's age which was forty-two in the fall of 1863. An unflattering description of Hagan appears in George Cary Eggleston's A Rebel's Recollections. Branded as a hairy giant with only his grotesque appearance to recommend him to Stuart who, according to Eggleston, was supposedly enamored of such things, Hagan has suffered much at the hands of writers and historians (none of whom ever took the time to verify Eggleston's claims). In actuality Hagan was a competent soldier who after Stuart's death joined the staff of Wade Hampton with whom he served until the end of the war. Hagan's postwar career included several years as the president of a cement works, hardly the position for an illiterate buffoon. Hagan died on June 18, 1895 and is buried in Elmwood Cemetery in Shepherdstown, West Virginia. (George Cary Eggleston, A Rebel's Recollections, pp. 128-129.)

8   Maj. Henry Brainerd McClellan had become Stuart's adjutant in May 1863 after the resignation of Maj. James Thomas Watt Hairston due to illness. McClellan had Northern roots having been born and raised in Philadelphia where his father and uncle, the father of Federal Maj. Gen. George B. McClellan, had founded Jefferson Medical College. His choice to throw his lot with the Confederacy came after just a little over two years in Virginia where he taught school. McClellan certainly vies for the honor of being the most intelligent and best educated member of the staff, having left high school at thirteen to attend Williams College in Massachusetts. He graduated at the age of seventeen with four degrees. His postwar career also involved education as he was headmaster of the Sayre Female Institute in Lexington, Kentucky for thirty-four years. He died on October 1, 1904 and is buried in Lexington Cemetery.

9   Rosser captured eight wagons loaded with ordnance stores, seven ambulances, two hundred and thirty horses and mules, took ninety-five prisoners and burned an additional thirty-five to forty wagons according to his report.

   Pvt. Channing Meade Smith was one of Stuart's and Robert E. Lee's most experienced and trusted scouts. Daring to the extreme, Smith roamed behind Federal lines to gather much needed information, often joining the Yanks for dinner where he learned much and enjoyed a free meal as well. He was a member of the 4th Virginia Cavalry's Company H and later rode with Col. John Singleton Mosby's Partisan Rangers rising to the rank of lieutenant.

   Pvt. Marcus A. Chewning accompanied Smith on several of the scout's missions. He had enlisted in the 9th Virginia Cavalry's Company E in April 1861. The fact that Smith chose Chewning to accompany him gives ample evidence to the courage and coolheadedness Chewning must have possessed.

10 Private Washington Nelson Toler was in the 6th Virginia Cavalry's Company K and was serving in the capacity of scout while attached to cavalry headquarters.

There were two Private George Woodbridges who served with Stuart during the war — George N. Woodbridge of the 4th Virginia Cavalry's Company I and George Woodbridge of Company E of the same regiment. As the dates of their service with Stuart are unknown it is difficult to know which individual Garnett mentions here. A "George Woodbridge" also appears in several of R. Channing Price's letters, but as in this case it is impossible to identify which one.

11 Stuart's report for the operations of his command from November 26 to December 3 substantiate the major facts of Garnett's narrative including the cross country march, Channing Smith's reporting to Stuart, and the gallantry of Rosser in the action at Parker's Store.

12 Capt. Hugh Holmes McGuire commanded Company E of the 11th Virginia Cavalry. He was mortally wounded at High Bridge on April 5, 1865 and died on May 8, 1865. He is buried in Stonewall Cemetery in Winchester, Virginia.

13 The date on which Stuart discovered that the Federals had withdrawn was December 2, 1863.

14 Capt William Willis Blackford had been Stuart's engineer officer since June 24, 1862. Born on March 23, 1831 Blackford had been a civil engineer before the war. A member of the Washington Mounted Rifles, which became Company D of the 1st Virginia Cavalry, Blackford became the regiment's adjutant under Stuart shortly before the Battle of 1st Manassas. In February 1864 he attained the rank of major, but with it came a transfer to the newly organizing engineer regiments. He had a distinguished postwar career and died on April 30, 1905. He is buried in Sinking Spring Cemetery in Abingdon, Virginia.

15 Garnett's memory was quite good. Only one line is in error. The third line of the second verse should read, "When through the invaders ranks they're crushing." (Blackford Papers, University of Virginia)

16 Sgt. Benjamin Weller enlisted in the 1st Virginia Cavalry's Company E in May 1861. Weller obviously had served under Stuart when he was colonel of the regiment. The earliest record of Weller's having joined cavalry headquarters is November 1862. He served first as a courier and later acted as chief of couriers. He had been wounded in action on November 27, 1863.

The identity of the Sergeant Buckner mentioned by Garnett is unknown.

17 Maj. Andrew Reid Venable, a native of Prince Edward County, Virginia, had joined the staff as assistant adjutant-general in May 1863 (to replace Maj. R. Channing Price who was killed at Chancellorsville) just a few days after Maj. H. B. McClellan, who outranked Venable by only nine days. Venable had known Stuart from meeting him in St. Louis in the Spring of 1855 while "Lieutenant" Stuart of the U.S. Cavalry was stationed at Jefferson Barracks, Missouri. At first a member of the 3rd Richmond Howitzers Venable received a commission as captain in the commissary department. At Chancellorsville Stuart and Venable renewed their friendship. Venable's performance under Stuart that day so impressed the cavalry chief that he had him transferred to his staff. As he lay dying Stuart left one of his horses, "General," to Venable. The other went to McClellan. After the war Venable settled down on his estate "Milnwood" near Farmville, Virginia. As a farmer he was not only successful but brought new innovations into the dairy industry of the area. He died on October 15, 1909 and was buried in Hampden-Sidney, Virginia.

18 Capt. Charles Grattan came from a distinguished Virginia family of Albemarle and Rock-ingham Counties. Early in the war Grattan became assistant quartermaster under Maj. John A. Harman, "Stonewall" Jackson's quartermaster. He then served one term in the state legislature as representative from Rockingham County. He joined Stuart as ordnance officer in October 1863. After Stuart's death Grattan first served on Wade Hampton's staff and later Fitzhugh Lee's. When the war ended he became a farmer in Augusta County, Virginia, but only for a short time. He resumed his law practice in 1871 in Staunton where he died on June 20, 1902. He was laid to rest in Thorn-rose Cemetery in Staunton.

    Capt. John Esten Cooke, a relative of Stuart's by marriage, preceded Grattan as the cavalry's ordnance officer. Recognizing that Cooke's real talent lay in writing Stuart transferred him to the adjutant-general's department and put him to work writing reports. Cooke, who idolized Stuart, wrote profusely after the war immortalizing Stuart and many of those who rode with him. An author at heart, Cooke was much more comfortable with the pen than the sword. His postwar career as a farmer was not very successful, but his writing supplemented his family's income. Cooke died of typhoid fever on September 27, 1886 and was buried in Old Chapel Cemetery in Clarke County, Virginia.

    Although coming from a wealthy background, which would have permitted him to avoid military service, Dr. John Boursiquot Fontaine chose to use his vast medical talents for the Confederacy. He joined the 4th Virginia Cavalry as regimental surgeon. His first wounded patient was his older brother, Edmund, whom he could not save. Fontaine replaced Surgeon Talcott Eliason in October 1863 and bore the heavy respon-sibilities of surgeon to the cavalry corps while not yet twenty-five. Upon Stuart's death he continued as chief surgeon of the cavalry under Hampton. Fontaine was killed in the line of duty on October 1, 1864. He is buried in the family cemetery at Beaver Dam, Virginia.

19 Grenfell is one of only three officers on Stuart's staff who has been the subject of a detailed biography (John Esten Cooke and John Pelham are the other two). A Britisher by birth and an adventurer by choice Grenfell fought, according to his account, in at least two wars prior to his arrival in the Confederacy. Obtaining a letter of introduction from no less a personage than John Slidell of the "Trent Affair," Grenfell made his way to Richmond where he seemingly impressed Gen. Robert E. Lee who sent him on to the western theater of operations. His association with Brig. Gen. John Hunt Morgan began soon after his arrival. Grenfell eventually returned to Virginia and assumed the post of the cavalry's inspector general. He was not well liked by some of the staff officers, but there is no evidence that Stuart treated him unfairly. His time with Stuart was very short and he left the Confederacy soon afterward. Journeying to Canada he became involved in the conspiracy to free Confederate prisoners incarcerated in Chicago. Captured, tried, and imprisoned in the Dry Tortugas he drowned during an escape attempt on the night of March 6-7, 1868. His body was never recovered.

20 Pvt. William M. Pegram was a member of the 4th Virginia Cavalry's Company H and was attached to Stuart's headquarters as a clerk for Maj. H.B. McClellan.

    Pvt. William R. Berkeley came from Company K of the 3rd Virginia Cavalry and served at headquarters as a clerk.

    Pvt. James Grant's magnificent bass contributed significantly to the headquarters "Amateur Glee-Club." He had been detached from the 10th Virginia Cavalry's Com-pany A and served as a clerk.

    Many and varied are the stories on Pvt. Sampson D. Sweeney of the 2nd Virginia Cavalry's Company H and how he came to ride with Stuart. His banjo playing won for him a considerable amount of immortality, but he was not the instrument's inven-tor as some credit him. His older brother, Joel W. Sweeney, should rightfully be given the recognition. Sam's actual duties while attached to cavalry headquarters are unclear, but it is certain that Stuart utilized him in ways other than banjo picking. Sweeney's date of death from smallpox was January 13, 1864.

    Pvt. Robert M. Sweeney also came from Company H of the 2nd Virginia Cavalry. His headquarters service is also unknown, but he did play the fiddle in the headquarters "band."

21   Maj. (later Lt. Col.) Johann August Heinrich Heros von Borcke served on Stuart's staff as assistant adjutant and inspector general. From Prussia, "Von," as he was called by Stuart and his fellow staff officers, was a very popular member of cavalry headquarters who in the postwar period claimed in his writings deeds which others of the staff had performed. While this ruffled a few feathers it did not destroy the friendship and camaraderie that had been formed during the war. Von Borcke was not present as a staff officer during the winter of 1863-64 having been gravely wounded at the Battle of Middleburg on June 19, 1863. On a mission in England for the Confederate government when the war ended, von Borcke returned to Prussia where he briefly reentered the army. The death of his father brought him the family estates which made him fairly wealthy. He returned to Virginia in 1884 for a whirlwind tour. He shocked his friends somewhat by his size having ballooned to over four hundred pounds. He died in Berlin on May 10, 1895.

22   Gen. Samuel Cooper was the ranking general in the Confederacy and served as its adjutant and inspector general. He never held field command.

    Lt. Chiswell Dabney joined Stuart's headquarters as a courier in December 1861 at the young age of seventeen. He became one of Stuart's aides on January 14, 1862. He accompanied Stuart to Verdiersville on August 18, 1862 when Stuart was almost captured. Following a promotion that made room for Garnett, Dabney served first with Brig. Gen. James B. Gordon and later with Brig. Gen. Rufus Barringer. After the war he practiced law for several years but in 1900 became a priest in the Episcopal Church. He died on April 28, 1923 and is buried in Chatham Cemetery, Chatham, Virginia.

    Garnett failed to include the second paragraph of Stuart's letter to Cooper which read, "It is proper that I should state that this recommendation is made from a knowledge of Private Garnett's gallantry in action, — irreproachable character and qualifications for the appointment."

23   The horse to which Garnett refers was procured during the Gettysburg Campaign before the cavalry reached Hanover, Pennsylvania. Lt. (later Capt.) Frank Smith Robertson, Stuart's assistant engineer, and Garnett found themselves in need of fresh mounts. They left the cavalry column and ventured into a nearby wood where they discovered several horses hidden from the Confederates to prevent exactly what took place. After the exchange the two horse traders returned to the column of gray cavalry. Lieutenant Robertson recorded that his horse gave out four days later. Apparently Garnett had been a better judge of horseflesh at least on that day. (see "Reminiscence Of the Years 1861-1865" by Capt. Frank S. Robertson, *The Historical Society of Washington County, VA. Bulletin*, Series II, No. 23, 1986)

24   "Lily of the Valley" had been presented to Stuart by Maj. James T. W. Hairston who had served as assistant adjutant general on the staff from January 16, 1862 to March 1, 1863. He was one of Stuart's many relatives who held positions on the staff at various times throughout the war.

    "Virginia" was from Maryland and had been used extensively in the Gettysburg Campaign. On June 30, 1863 at Hanover, Pennsylvania, "Virginia" saved her rider's life by jumping a wide ditch with Union troopers in close pursuit.

    "My Maryland" (in the text shortened to "Maryland" by Garnett) was the gift of Stuart's Maryland troopers. He rode the bay on his excursion around McClellan's army to Chambersburg. Stuart could not help scripting a new verse to fit his gallant steed.

"Your master's heel is in your flank,
Maryland, My Maryland.
I hear his restless saber clank,
Maryland, My Maryland
He'll ride you hard and you may thank
Your lucky stars, if not left lean and lank,
Without the rations due your rank,
Maryland, My Maryland

I feel secure upon your back,
Maryland, My Maryland
When cannon roar and rifle crack,
Maryland, My Maryland
You bore me o'er the Po-to-mac,
You circumvented 'Little Mac,'
Oh may I never know your lack,
Maryland, My Maryland"

"My Maryland" was reported to have been the only horse Stuart owned that was gentle enough for his wife, Flora, to ride.

"Star of the East" was from Fauquier County and was presented to Stuart by one of his aides.

The iron gray Garnett mentions here was called "General" and was the horse Venable received from the dying Stuart.

Glanders is a contagious disease caused by a germ which enters the system most easily when the animal is debilitated. The symptoms are refusal of food, rough coat, perspiration at the slightest exertion, a discharge of a gluey material mixed with blood from one or both nostrils, and enlargement of the glands under the jaw which gives the disease its name. The disease is fatal and is communicable to humans.

25 Lt. James E. Webb was assistant ordnance officer to Capt. Charles Grattan. He was from Alabama and later served with Brig. Gen. James Dearing's Cavalry Brigade as ordnance officer.

26 Maj. (later Col.) John S. Mosby, onetime scout attached to Stuart's headquarters, had by this time established himself as a successful partisan ranger commander. His relationship with Stuart was very close, and after the war Mosby championed Stuart when others turned against him for his role in the Gettysburg Campaign.

27 Pvt. Mathew Polk Burke of Company F, 1st Virginia Cavalry was the son of the famous scout Captain Redmond Burke of Stuart's staff who had been killed in an ambush in Shepherdstown, West Virginia, on the night of November 24-25, 1862. His son evidently followed in his father's footsteps as a scout for Stuart.

Pvt. Benjamin Franklin Stringfellow originally served with Company E of the 4th Virginia Cavalry. Daring to the point of foolhardiness Stringfellow carved a reputation as a scout second to none during the war. Accused in the postwar era of embellishing his record with extravagant claims, if only half of his adventures were only half truths he would still be one of Stuart's and Robert E. Lee's finest scouts. He became a minister after the war.

Pvt. Washington N. Toler was detached to cavalry headquarters from the 6th Virginia Cavalry's Company K.

Pvt. Charles P. Curtis of the 4th Virginia Cavalry's Company H specialized in scouting in Fauquier County.

28 Garnett was in error. The horse artillery encamped near Charlottesville was under the temporary command of Capt. Marcellus Newton Moorman, not Breathed. (Maj. Robert

Franklin Beckham had recently been promoted and transferred.) Capt. James Breathed was the commander of one of the horse batteries there and would later command a battalion of the horse artillery under Maj. (later Lt. Col.) Roger Preston Chew. Breathed was from Maryland and owed his appointment to the horse artillery to a train ride with Stuart when the two were returning east just prior to the war. Once he attained his position, however, Breathed needed no one's help to hold it. He proved to be one of the finest horse artillery officers in the Army of Northern Virginia and garnered accolades from every superior he served under as well as Gen. Robert E. Lee himself. Breathed was a physician in the postwar. He died at Hancock, Maryland, on February 14, 1870 and is buried there in St. Thomas Episcopal Church Cemetery.

29   Pvt. Augustine Henry Ellis had been a member of Company H of the 13th Virginia Cavalry before being attached to Stuart's headquarters as a courier.
        The "Brofford" referred to by Garnett was actually Private James Brawford of the 10th Virginia Cavalry's Company B who was detached to cavalry headquarters as a courier.
        Pvt. George Freed had enlisted in the Valley Rangers on April 19, 1861 and soon found himself in Company E of the 1st Virginia Cavalry. Then Col. J.E.B. Stuart had Freed attached to his headquarters as bugler where he stayed until Stuart's death.
        Pvt. Alexander Speirs George was from the 10th Virginia Cavalry's Company A, and prior to his service as a courier for Stuart he had been a member of Stuart's escort.

30   The incident mentioned here occurred on the morning of August 18, 1862 when Stuart, expecting to rendezvous with Fitz Lee, was visited instead by the 1st Michigan Volunteer Cavalry. The interlopers captured Stuart's adjutant, Maj. Norman Richard FitzHugh, and several pieces of Stuart's clothing including his cloak, talma, and hat not to mention General Lee's orders to Stuart involving plans for his upcoming offensive against Maj. Gen. John Pope which were with Major FitzHugh. (John W. Thomason, Jr., *Jeb Stuart*, pp. 222-224; Heros von Borcke, *Memoirs of the Confederate War*, pp. 104-108)

31   Lt. Robert E. Lee, Jr. was then serving as aide-de-camp on the staff of Major General William Henry Fitzhugh "Rooney" Lee.

32   The side notation of a question mark would seem to indicate that someone thought that an error may have been made in reference to which of Hooker's flanks Jackson had surprised. Garnett himself may have written the question mark with the intention of later verifying his text, but there is no way to determine if this was the case. In any event it was Hooker's right flank.

33   Brig. Gen. Hugh Judson Kilpatrick began his famous raid on Richmond on February 28, 1864. Accompanying him was Colonel Ulric Dahlgren and about 3,500 cavalry. The plan was to ride into Richmond and free Union prisoners of war held there. The raid failed, and Dahlgren was shot on March 2, 1864 by Lieutenant James Pollard of the 9th Virginia cavalry.
        Brig. Gen. George A. Custer's role in Kilpatrick's scheme was one of diversion. He was repulsed at the Battle of Rio Hill near Charlottesville by about two hundred men of the Stuart Horse Artillery.

34   The "Atwell" referred to in the text was most likely Capt. W.H. Atwell, assistant commissary of subsistence, on the staff of Maj. Gen. Henry Heth who was undoubtedly the "General H." of Garnett's anecdote.

35   That cavalry headquarters was dismantled on May 4, 1864 is corroborated by the diary of Col. Alexander R. Boteler, volunteer aide-de-camp to Stuart. (*Southern Cavalry Review*, Vol. VI, No. 6, May 1989, newsletter of the Stuart-Mosby Historical Society)

36   The brush with disaster that Garnett recorded could well have put a quick end to the war. With Gen. Robert E. Lee dead or a prisoner and a number of the other high

ranking officers of the army killed, wounded or captured the Army of Northern Virginia would have been hard pressed to recover. (see the diary of Col. Alexander R. Boteler *Southern Cavalry Review*, Vol. VI, No. 6, May 1989; and Douglas Southall Freeman, *R.E. Lee* Vol. III, p. 278.)

37   Lt. Col. Charles S. Venable, assistant adjutant general, and Lt. Col. Walter H. Taylor, assistant adjutant general, are the officers of Gen. Lee's staff whom Garnett mentions.

38   The near catastrophe described by Garnett was not caused by a brigade retiring too early, but rather by the confusion caused by the hard fighting that day. The divisions of Maj. Gen. Cadmus M. Wilcox and Maj. Gen. Henry Heth had become intermingled during the fight. Both generals made attempts to persuade their superior, Lt. Gen. A. P. Hill, to allow them to realign their commands but were refused on the grounds that the men were tired and should not be disturbed. The Federal attack that followed routed both Wilcox's and Heth's divisions and was only halted and driven back when Lieutenant General James Longstreet Corps reached the field and counterattacked.

    Col. Alexander R. Boteler mentioned in his diary that Stuart and his staff helped to rally some retreating troops on the evening of the May 6, but fails to identify them. By all appearances Garnett remembered various events that happened over the course of the two days (May 5-6), but as he stated he "could not pretend to a sufficientcy [sic] of knowledge or accuracy of recollection to give any detailed account of these fights." This is especially true of his comments concerning the various infantry units engaged with which he was unfamiliar. (see the diary of Col. Alexander R. Boteler *Southern Cavalry Review*, Vol. VI, No. 6, May 1989.)

39   Garnett was mistaken here. Stevens did not reach the rank of brigadier general until August 28, 1864. At the time of the Wilderness he was a colonel.

40   Pvt. Charles D. Lownes belonged to Company E, 4th Virginia Cavalry and was attached to cavalry headquarters as a courier.

41   The episode which Garnett failed to describe in detail was undoubtedly Breathed's finest moment in the war. The gun's placement made it the primary target of the advancing Union infantry, and after giving the bluecoats several rounds the gunners decided that the situation demanded their immediate withdrawal. Breathed received an order to pull out but begged to be allowed a few more shots. Soon the enemy was so close their shouts could be heard above the musketry. Called on to surrender, the cannoneers abandoned the gun, mounted their horses and headed rearward. But Breathed was not about to lose the piece. His own horse having already been shot beneath him, he mounted a lead horse after limbering the gun singlehandedly. The lead horse too went down. Cutting the harness of the leaders with his knife Breathed leaped upon one of the swing horses and galloped from the field in the direction of the road. Just as he was turning into the road the swing horse he was riding was hit. Again he severed the harness, mounted one of the wheel horses and brought the gun back to Confederate lines through a shower of Yankee bullets and cheers.

    It is important to note that Breathed was still a captain at this time. He was promoted to major on May 22, 1864.

42   Coxe's account of the fighting that day presents a close look at Stuart's and his staff's role in the battle that does not vary to any degree from what Garnett recorded.

43   Both Privates A.J. Shepherd and Alexander Hunter survived their wounds. Hunter was also a member of the "Black Horse" which was Company H of the 4th Virginia Cavalry.

44   Maj. Gen. Richard H. Anderson had replaced Lt. Gen. James Longstreet on the May 6 when the latter was severely wounded by a volley from his own men. Having march-

ed to Spotsylvania Court House to relieve the cavalry under Fitz Lee, Anderson found his situation desperate. The Federals were lengthening their line on his right flank, and he could not stretch his to cover their move. Garnett's recollection of this crucial time is accurate except that the infantry on the extreme flank was not Hay's Louisiana Brigade which was part of Maj. Gen. Jubal A. Early's Division of the Second Corps. Anderson only had Brig. Gen. Joseph B. Kershaw's and Maj. Gen. Charles W. Field's Divisions with him at that time.

45   Stuart expressed similar words to one of his adjutants, Maj. Andrew R. Venable, as they were riding away from Col. Edmund Fontaine's plantation near Beaver Dam Station on May 10. The general had stopped there to visit his wife, Flora, before moving on in pursuit of Sheridan.

46   Other accounts, most notably Maj. Henry B. McClellan's, state that Gordon was with Stuart and Fitz Lee when they joined Brig. Gen. Williams C. Wickham at Mitchell's Shop. It is doubtful that Garnett is in error as his meeting and return with Gordon to Chilesburg are presented with such detail, and it does not differ materially in time or distance from McClellan's.

47   Gordon's Brigade crossed the North Anna River at Davenport's Bridge which is west of the route taken by Fitz Lee.

48   Garnett refers to the three Hebrews who, according to the book of Daniel in the Old Testament, were thrown into a fiery furnace by King Nebuchadnezzar and emerged unharmed.

49   This battery was also known as the 2nd Maryland Battery and was part of the Stuart Horse Artillery Battalion. Stuart picked up the battery at Hanover Junction on the way to Yellow Tavern as Garnett relates. In doing so Stuart promised Col. Bradley T. Johnson, commanding the Maryland Line to which the battery was then attached, that he would borrow the battery for a few days and return it in good condition. Originally commanded by John Bowyer Brockenbrough the battery was led at Yellow Tavern by Capt. Wiley Hunter Griffin who was captured and spent the remainder of the war a prisoner. His battery lost two of its four guns and several men were casualties. Griffin became a business man in Texas after the war. He died in Galveston on November 23, 1896 and was buried in City Cemetery.

50   The date refers to the day and year Garnett again began to write.

51   Stuart had visited Pate earlier in the battle. They had been at odds with each other but during this meeting had made amends. At this time Stuart had told Pate he must hold his position until reinforcements arrived. Garnett's mission to Pate came just prior to a renewed Federal advance when Stuart realized additional troops would not be available to support Pate's line. Pate was killed in the attack that followed.

52   Lt. William Hoxton commanded a section in Capt. Philip Preston Johnston's 1st Stuart Horse Artillery formerly commanded by John Pelham and then James Breathed. He would be wounded at Trevilian Station later in the war. He survived to become a minister in postwar Virginia and died in Richmond on May 31, 1876. He is buried in Hollywood Cemetery.

53   "Old Carpenter" was probably Pvt. A.H. Carpenter of Company C of the 4th Virginia Cavalry.
     Apparently at the time of Stuart's wounding not a single staff officer was with him. He was assisted from his horse by Capt. Gustavus W. Dorsey of Company K, 1st Virginia Cavalry and lay on the ground for several minutes. Then Stuart was helped to remount "General," the gray he was riding that day, and led to the rear. The horse, not used to being led, became unmanageable, and Stuart was again helped to the ground and

placed with his back against a tree. Pvt. Frederick. L. Pitts of Dorsey's company brought his horse. For the second time Stuart was assisted to mount and taken from the field where he was in danger of being captured. From all that can be ascertained concerning the shooting the man who fired the fatal bullet was Pvt. John A. Huff of Company E, 5th Michigan Cavalry, formerly of the Berdan Sharpshooters.

54 Archibald C. Randolph was the surgeon attached to the 1st Virginia Cavalry.

55 The funeral was held on May 13. Others who acted as pall-bearers were Brigadier Generals John H. Winder and Alexander R. Lawton, former Secretary of War, George W. Randolph and Commodore French Forrest.

56 Pvt. William T. Thompson had been attached to Stuart's headquarters from Company G of the 13th Virginia Cavalry.

57 Lee was suffering from some intestinal malady which he contracted on the night of the 23-24 or May 24. He accompanied Lt. Gen. Richard S. Ewell's Corps toward Richmond on the May 27, and due to his illness he did not ride Traveller but chose a conveyance of some kind. Exactly what Lee rode in is not known so Garnett's recollection of seeing Lee in an ambulance can be accepted as accurate.

58 Lt. Col. John MacPherson Millen of the 20th Battalion Georgia Partisan Rangers was the officer killed at Haw's Shop.

59 Of these officers Maj. Luke Tiernan Brien and Lt. Frank S. Robertson had also been officers on Stuart's staff. Brien had been one of the first three officers Stuart appointed to his staff upon becoming a brigadier general. Robertson had been assistant engineer officer under Captain William W. Blackford. Lt. Beverly B. Turner was a brother of Lt. Thomas Baynton Turner who had been one of Stuart's aides-de-camp before joining John S. Mosby's partisan rangers with whom he was killed in a small skirmish. The commissary officer that Garnett could not remember was Maj. Albert G. Dade.

60 Lt. Charles Edward Ford of Fairfax Courthouse, Virginia, commanded a section of guns in Capt. William Morrell McGregor's 2nd Stuart Horse Artillery. He was the brother of Antonia Ford who was arrested by Union forces as a Confederate spy. Lieutenant Ford's remains were later recovered and reinterred in Hollywood Cemetery in Richmond, Virginia.

61 The action to which Garnett refers took place on April 6, 1865. The Federal officer who engaged in the pistol duel with Dearing was Brigadier General Theodore Read not "Rice" as Garnett states (Garnett may have confused the name of the officer with the name of the small railroad station, Rice's Depot, which was about four and a half miles south of High Bridge). Read was killed almost instantly, and Dearing died of his wound on April 23, 1865, the last Confederate general officer to die from wounds received in battle.

62 The Wilson-Kautz Raid took place between June 22 and July 1, 1864. The raiders failed to accomplish anything permanent (the sixty odd miles of railroad they destroyed were repaired in a short time) and were eventually attacked at Ream's Station as they tried to return to their own lines. After suffering about 1,500 casualties, losing all twelve of their guns, and having to burn their wagon train the remnants of the Federal cavalry returned to the safety of their infantry.